Tony Smith

# Parzival's Briefcase

## Six Practices
## and a New Philosophy
## for Healthy Organizational
## Change

Illustrations by Anthony Russo

Chronicle Books    San Francisco

Printed in the United States of America.

Library of Congress Cataloging-in-Publication Data

Smith, Tony.

    Parzival's briefcase: six practices and a new philosophy for healthy
organizational change / Tony Smith.

      p. cm.

    Includes index.

    ISBN 0-8118-0061-X

    1. Organizational change. 2. Organizational effectiveness. I. Title.

HD58.8.S64 1993                 92-22649

658.4'063—dc20                   CIP

Book and cover design: Rob Hugel, XXX Design

Cover illustration: Anthony Russo

Distributed in Canada by Raincoast Books,
112 East Third Avenue, Vancouver, B.C. V5T 1C8

10 9 8 7 6 5 4 3 2 1

Chronicle Books
275 Fifth Street
San Francisco, CA 94103

To Ralph Smith, Jane Porter, and Doug Smith

**Acknowledgments.**

Nobody actually writes a book alone. I didn't. Friends
supported me, urged me to keep at it, objected when I
slowed down, and provided insights. Several of them were
secret heroes whom I thought of as I wrote: Lillian Conrad,
John Pekrul, George Porter, Julia McHugh, David Baker,
Bob Prokop, Scott Orlosky, Doug Crase, Heidi Ellison,
Christine Taylor, Gary Stewart, and George Clark made
the book possible.

The people with whom I worked taught me what needs
to be done to make a difference in the world and how to
go about doing it. They constantly enlarged my understanding of what is possible and they inspired me. These people
are: Cheryl French, Sam Taylor, and Dorothy Miller.

Others were models. They are professional change
agents, although they don't necessarily think of themselves
that way, who are masters of their craft. I watched them
work, admired what they did, and wrote them into the book:
Kelly Poulos, Alan Lemon, J.C. Green, and Dennis
Ranahan.

The people at Chronicle Books are consummate
professionals. I am grateful to my editor, Jay Schaefer, for
helping to bring this book into being, and to Karen Silver in
the editorial department and to Sharon Silva for her
copyediting.

It is a pleasure to thank these people.

# Table of Contents

TABLE OF CONTENTS

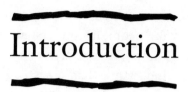

# Introduction

We live in revolutionary times and our lives are being altered in ways we cannot predict. Every major institution is being transformed. Our most deeply held values are in dispute and the nature of personal relationships is changing drastically. Our capacity to feed and house ourselves, to live healthy and useful lives, to work productively with one another, and to pass on a decent world to our children is in doubt. So anyone who wants to generate meaningful responses to the events of the times must become a change agent.

Only those who have moved into personal alignment with these challenges will do this work well. Those who assume they can cause other people and organizations to change while they themselves stand still will not be effective. Their understanding of the new forces will be inadequate. Their decisions will be unrealistic.

The life force of organizational change is personal change. People who are changing in order to live productively in this new age can create extraordinary results. They will invent unexpected solutions to oppressive problems and generate a dialogue that produces new ways for people to understand the world and to work effectively together. The key element in this dynamic is a particular turn of mind. More than amassed capital or technological knowledge, more than accumulated wisdom or powerful connections, a flexible and inventive approach to life will determine who recognizes new resources and transforms them into useful goods, services, and values. Only those who venture to the edge of what we understand, hold the light up, and take action will succeed.

For twenty years I have worked with people who are interested in being as effective as possible, and the most successful change agents I have encountered in this time are moved by an expansive vision. They are fascinated by life and driven to experience it fully. They respond well to change although they do not necessarily like it. They think clearly when information is uncertain and structures of belief are impaired. They see connections between a fast-moving world and their organization, and they have an open and receptive state of mind that is not paralyzed by information they had not expected or did not want to see. They have mastered the difficult art of working well with people and are able to communicate honestly, pursue a compelling vision, and engage with integrity.

I have watched them learn that they must be fully committed to change, that modest change efforts do not have a lasting impact. I have seen them discover that they cannot manipulate or force other people or institutions to change. But *they* can change and evolve, move deftly and invent. They can become catalysts for genuine personal and organizational transformation.

The assertion that change agents should work this way is unsettling to many people. They feel that making deep changes is unrealistic, that only romantics try it. They warn about soft-headed optimism and speak of the limits of change. But real problems will not be solved by tough-guy posturing. And what is truly soft headed is to think that if you do not understand something or do not like it, you should ignore it, trivialize it, or stomp it to death.

A powerful resistance always thrives during times of transition and it is pervasive today. Leaders are not making the difficult decisions that are needed; organizations are not developing incisive transition strategies. Employee burnout and ineffectiveness are epidemic at a time when creativity, quality, and service are vitally important. Even those who advocate change have been recommending easy solutions they knew would not work, and couching their proposals in mild terms so that decision makers would not be offended and run away. But the time has come for us to talk to one another with candor and respect, to go to the edge together and take a good look.

We are ready to do it. Although we have spent a lot of time engaged in shadow change efforts that were overtaken by resistance and lassitude, we have learned from our failures, too. We know what genuine change looks like and what generates it. We know how to put together realistic programs that work. Because we are smack in the middle of transition, the genuinely new is more likely to emerge now.

To succeed at this, we will need to do away with the belief that we must only be logical, unemotional, and tough at work, and that passion, radical curiosity, and trust need to be suppressed. The idea that we stop being complete human beings when we put on a power tie and go to work is absurd. It creates unrealistic expectations and leads people to ignore some of their greatest gifts. For too long, people have been running away from themselves.

As a result of this flight, another romantic idea has developed: that modern life is a new kind of hell, that never before has humankind faced such rapid change, so many threats to its existence. So people laugh at attempts to bring about transitions that make human sense and vilify them as impractical. They are overwhelmed by their problems and decline to seek real solutions.

Yet human beings have always faced the sorts of problems we do today. In the course of millenia, a good many brilliant and rewarding ways of coming to grips with these problems have been developed. Responding adequately to the questions that animate our lives now doesn't require that we make up totally new responses. Wise and practical traditions are available to us if we will open up to them.

Part One of this book, The Philosopher's Road Map, describes two of these traditions. They present a program for moving with confidence and agility during times when the old guideposts no longer work. They help you create your own map for this territory of transformation. The first tradition you will use for your map comes in the form of mythology. The great myths teach us to look honestly at what ails us and to set about solving the problems we uncover. They offer guidance in handling tension and conflict, finding resources where none appear to be, and living productively with disappointment and doubt. They tell us how to invent and create when we are tired and frightened, how to work effectively with people we may not understand or like, and how to persevere in the face of daunting odds. They tell us how to do all this more clearly and compellingly than any work manual can.

The second tradition—philosophy—guides us in looking honestly at ourselves in the unexpected world we have come to inhabit. It is the discipline that shows us how to understand this map. If we can learn to read our deepest responses to what a changing world presents, we can use this knowledge as a gauge for what to do next. This tells us how to determine what is actually happening as opposed to what we want to see. It tells us how to decide what is genuinely possible, what we can do about it, and what is beyond our means. It has provided profound and practical direction to people living in transitional times for thousands of years.

Part Two, Six Practices, presents a strategy for taking effective action. It describes six essential practices that have proved to be the most effective for change agents: Discover Your Vision, Understand Your Intention, Work with Integrity, Participate Fully in Your Life, Express Yourself, and Create Knowledge-Based Relationships. Each practice specifies methods for staying alert, responsive, and creative during the process of making deep changes. They teach you how to notice emerging forces quickly, how to communicate what you see, and how to build power and support.

Part Three, Enduring Value, lays out a plan for building strong and resilient organizations. It contains information about the social laws of groups that determine what strategies will succeed, what it takes for people to work creatively and cohesively together, and how to build an organization that will remain in fruitful touch with its evolving environment.

This book grew out of my experiences with people engaged in change efforts in the workplace. It is the story of how these complex, maddening, and extraordinary people think, and what they do when change is in the air. It is an account of what works and what does not, a map for leaders who want to establish new directions, for managers who will implement new programs, for employees who will make the final difference, and for others who simply care a lot. It urges change agents to look at themselves, organizational cultures, and personal relations in all their complexity, not through cleaned-up models, checklists, and canned procedures.

This book is a guide to taking direct action, and I hope you use it that way. But its ultimate purpose is to assist you and the organizations you care about to find an authentic voice. To follow its recommendations is to begin a journey toward self-knowledge, to come out of hiding and move along the edge of possibility. It is to experience the joys and sorrows of being who you really are and to create work groups that are human centered, action oriented, and focused on results. It is to build organizations that may be relied upon and trusted, that invent effective responses to serious problems, and where loyalty and intimacy are possible and people are not dominated by fear.

# I

# The Philosopher's Road Map

# 1

## Understanding Change

Change is *the* fact of life. Although we often think nostalgically of the past as a pleasant, slow-moving affair where people lived in hospitable communities that cherished family values and simple truths, that is not the way our ancestors usually saw things. Pick up almost any history book that reports their actual words and you will see something familiar: people as stunned by the way life turns out as we are.

They talk about how things have never been so bad and they cannot keep up with the changes. They describe military invasions, economic dislocation, disease, and natural disasters that changed their lives beyond recognition. They did not know what to do about these troubles any more than we do.

Some who observed these phenomena were more sanguine about it, however. For thousands of years, philosophers have said that significant change is the rule not the exception in human life. Aristotle, for example, said that the core of human life, the first cause of everything, is *dynamus*, or "becoming." These observers make it clear that like it or not, understand it or not, we and everything we love in this world are in constant transition, in the act of becoming. When we acknowledge a change in our circumstances and move to meet it, we are realigning ourselves with the rhythms of the changing world.

Sometimes this process scarcely seems like change at all. It may appear to be an orderly and dignified road through the life cycle, a progressive movement from conception to birth, from youth to maturity, and then to old age. Change can mean evolution. It can be a welcome gift, bringing release and replenishment. But it can also be sudden and violent. This is the form we tend to know it by when we are caught in the midst of transition.

However we experience it, change inevitably comes to us whether we want it to or not. If we wait long enough, it will alter everything in our world. The only real question about change is whether we participate actively in it. This becomes particularly clear when small changes periodically accumulate, and larger shifts need to occur if people and organizations are going to shake loose from antiquated ways in order to meet the needs of the day. In this situation responding to change is not simply a matter of finding methods for doing things better. These changes require fundamental alterations in the way relations are structured, the way we distribute resources, and in our beliefs about what is right and true. When accumulated rumblings and shifts gather force this way, an earthquake makes its way to the surface. We are experiencing the big one right now.

We live in a time of transition, one of those prime moments in history when a whole new economic, political, and cultural world is emerging. We are in the midst of a paradigm shift where the way in which we identify our values, laws, and relationships is changing dramatically. Confusion and conflict proliferate during these periods, and there are no widely acknowledged rules of the game to provide stability, confidence, and understanding.

In the United States, the old way of doing business is disintegrating and nearly every company is engaged in making significant changes. The factors that fuel this phenomenon include a technological revolution, powerful new international competition for markets and resources, new employee attitudes, and new consumer needs. *Fortune* magazine has written that we are in the midst of a transition as great as the one that followed the invention of the steam engine and electricity. The editor of *Harvard Business Review* has said that leading and managing have changed so drastically that managers are literally reinventing their profession on the job every day. No company is too small or too isolated to be unaffected by this state of affairs.

Major social institutions are also in trouble, unable to deliver the services expected of them, wondering where their next dollar will come from, uncertain about their responsibilities and span of influence. The problems they face and the solutions that are at hand for them are inextricably linked to those of business.

During times such as this, organizations and institutions must do more than tinker and adjust. They must transform themselves by developing new understandings of their contribution and locating new resources and networks of support. They must form effective relationships with an emerging and still to be defined environment.

Most of the organizations that prosper in this evolving landscape will be cohesive, inventive, and able to change quickly when the marketplace or the competition does. They will develop products and services that are genuinely needed and will deliver what they promise. They will be guided by leaders who know how to compel belief and are able to get the best out of their colleagues, who can create more powerful responses with fewer resources. Achieving this mix of qualities is not easy. But it must be done or the inventing and delivering of the new products, services, and values that are necessary now simply will not happen.

———

## When People Skills Are Not Enough

———

What usually happens in the early stages of a transitional era, however, is not deep organizational change at all. Instead, leaders tend to look at the first symptoms that appear and try to make them go away. Then problems fester, people suffer, productivity and work standards decline. Trust and focus are lost, and handling continuous conflict gains a new urgency. That is happening now, and most organizations spend more time dealing with "people problems" than they do inventing, producing, and serving.

Graduates of MBA programs regularly report that while they learn sufficient technical skills in school, they wish they had more training in "people skills," because the vast majority of their time is spent dealing with people. They say the outcomes of these human interactions determine whether or not they are able to apply their technical skills, that these interactions govern their success or failure and the future of their companies.

Many leaders respond to these newly recognized needs by altering their training and education activities. They set up programs to teach the skills of talking, listening, asserting, team building, negotiating, and being nice. But as valuable as these skills are, if they are not practiced in a context that is congenial to them, a transformed context where people are thinking and working honestly, directly, and effectively, their usefulness fades quickly, leaving frustration and lassitude in their wake.

That congenial context is rare. Most decision makers are uneasy about these programs, suspecting that their value is limited, so when the big quake hits a company, leaders usually stop the change activity immediately. They get "real and tough." They jump like scalded cats and go back to what they were doing all along.

Laura's company, a large East Coast corporation, has lots of people-skills programs. For years its leaders have worked to reduce conflict and promote communication. But recently they made some major changes that dwarfed these efforts. Realizing that the economy was not doing them any favors and reacting to crises in their industry, they instituted a plan that cut their executive staff in half, drastically slashed operating expenses, and lopped off several product lines. They did this in the interest of streamlining the bureaucracy, cutting the payroll, getting lean and mean and effective.

Although only a few executives were involved in developing the plan, everyone was involved in deciding who should stay and who should go. Employees were asked to report on other people's attitudes and abilities and to evaluate company needs against their colleagues' special skills. Peer review ran amok as decision makers sought to push the responsibility for their decisions down the ranks, and the employee-involvement programs and the people-skills trainings they had developed were used to make this strategy work.

The result of the peer review was predictable: the middle of the organization was ousted. Those between the ages of thirty and forty, middle managers, women, and minorities are mostly gone now. Those people who were seen as clogging the bureaucracy, who brought different perspectives that have to be brokered, are out looking for new jobs. But Laura survived and she is relieved. She hopes to see a new age of creativity and practical action emerge from this trauma.

Executing a monumental series of cuts in people and programs is an understandable tactic, and under some circumstances, it can be a wise one. But in this case the activity was generated neither by a thorough analysis of the situation nor an evaluation of the company's core assumptions or basic functions. It was not part of a long-term strategy. It was a reaction to a set of largely unanticipated events and it was administered awkwardly. It was a serious misuse of peer review that undermined cooperation, trust, and inventiveness.

When seismic shocks shake lots of people out of an organization, they send a compelling message to the survivors. It is a variation on the old theme of shut up and do your job. And although at first people may be encouraged—as Laura was—to seek the new creativity, the only creativity to flourish will be the sort that articulates the still powerful old paradigm. The survivors will grit their teeth, work harder and longer, and become rigid and positioned. They will need dozens of new people-skills courses.

This state of affairs produces a general malaise, a disengagement from one's self and the world, an inability to see and respond to what is emerging on the horizon. People will suppress any big questions that may begin to form in their minds, and most new ideas that come to them will not be communicated. Warnings they know are important to issue will be kept close to the vest, and they will do everything they can to fit in. From now on, when the emperor stops by their cubicle during a coffee break, stark staring pink, all shiny and naked, they are sure to say "Love your outfit."

These suicide change efforts are common during times of transition. When they come about, they obliterate all the efforts to teach people to work together harmoniously and creatively. They stop risk taking and invention. They make it difficult for the organization to take advantage of the radical creativity that is a part of any successful transition.

## The Problem with Elite Change Gangs

Another change method commonly employed with unsatisfactory results during the early stages of transition is the designation of a select group as the inventors. These people tend to be given better equipment, great perks, higher pay, and an exalted status. None of this means that their creativity will become a central aspect of organizational vision, strategy, or policy, however. Nor does it assure them a pleasant time of it. What it does do is produce a chasm between them and their colleagues.

Everyone in the organization needs to emerge from isolation, create connections, and develop new ways of going about things. A transitional culture is weakened when any one group is perceived as special, and an elite research team that does fabulous work while the rest of the organization continues to stagnate can create more problems than it solves. The majority of the people in any organization know this. They see how their bosses and the court favorites behave, they know that this activity often fails to produce useful results, and they are not impressed.

Creating special teams is often a way for leaders to convince themselves that they are responding to new challenges when they are actually only making gestures. Yet if leaders are prone to denial and gesturing in the face of an urgent need for organizational transformation, so are employees. One fear predominates in everybody's mind when this sort of crisis is at hand. This fear, which produces tough-guy posturing rather than genuine engagement with real problems, was put especially well one day by a clerk in an embattled company where I was working. He said, "If we do what you say and go around acting nice all the time, we'll get our lunches ate." He spoke for millions.

But who said anything about being nice? Taking a deep look, identifying what you do best, and learning how to cooperate, take risks, and invent is exacting work. Performing in this engaged fashion does not mean throwing out rational calculation, hard actions, and careful planning. And it gets real results, while an obsessive fear that your lunch will be eaten by someone else produces rigidity, suspicion, and other antic behaviors that are dysfunctional during transitions. You can live an open and inventive life and still bang anyone over the head who sneaks into your lunch bucket.

## The Stability of Human Culture

So why do leaders prefer gesturing to making deep changes when it is obvious to any observer that such behavior is foolish? Leaders get where they are and stay there not because they are adept at understanding change, but because they are masters of culture, or because powerful elements in the culture gave them this position and they are its symbol.

If life is constant change, human culture is stability. Culture is the body of accumulated expectations, beliefs, and perceptions that guides our lives. It organizes the ways in which we explain what happens to us. It brings order to chaos and allows us to feel that we know a thing or two, so that we can make a calculation or a prediction, and understand what life is all about. Without culture, human life would be impossible.

Culture sets the boundaries, determining what is real and what does not exist. It tells us what we should pay attention to and what is just noise, what is right and what is wrong, what is natural and what is unnatural, what is beautiful and what is disgusting. It is our understanding of how a mother or father should behave, and it is the music we enjoy. Culture is the way we express being human; it is deeply ingrained, passionately felt, and impervious to rational considerations. We will starve for culture, kill for it, and die for it.

Because culture is so powerful and all-encompassing, we do not identify its components as beliefs. We think of them simply as the way things are—as reality. And giving people who work in organizations that need a cultural overhaul better time-management techniques, computer training, or lessons on forming problem-solving teams is hilariously inadequate. Any change program that conflicts with the forces of an aroused culture will be left limp and bleeding.

## The Culture of Organizations

During normal times a leader's job is to perpetuate the culture of his or her organization. An organization's resources and activities are structured to produce goods, services, and values, and its culture guides every aspect of the process. Whatever else an organization does, its ultimate goal is to perpetuate its culture. Any change expert can relate gaudy stories about this culture-protecting phenomenon. It is pervasive and as old as the hills.

No organization is immune to this. An organization has all the properties of an organism. It is born with a genetic code that determines how it looks, what diseases it is susceptible to, and how it ages. It lives in an environment from which it receives challenges and takes sustenance. These are factors about which it can do very little. Internally an organization has a set of interdependent parts and processes that make it function. If one part changes, so will the others. The people in organizations cannot do much about this dynamic either.

The organizational functions people perform have much to do with how they think, feel, and behave. So when the structure of an organization changes, either the people in it change too or they begin to feel great discomfort. They begin to float, to wonder who they are in the absence of secure guideposts on how to act. People do not blithely will changes in this system on themselves. They will try any trick to avoid them.

Yet the forces of change, both inside and outside the organization, are in constant movement. They cannot be put off for long, and no amount of toughness, repression, or denial has ever worked to alter this fact. Those organisms that survive over time are the ones that develop mechanisms to incorporate these changes into their structures. But before they do, they will struggle to remain as they are, to protect the culture that determines their internal order and seems to hold off chaos.

Competent leaders are acutely aware of the power of this culture and cannot easily be convinced to alter it. Nor are they likely to want to. All they are seems to be connected with it. So when the best journals or popular literature reports that change is the name of the game, they may have a halfhearted go at it. But to transform the culture that created them is another thing entirely. That is an act of violence.

It is one of the ironies of human life that when people most need to be open and inventive, they're usually totally frightened. They become rigid. They feel an overwhelming need to be right about things, even unimportant things. They are anxious to appear rational and logical, to assure people that they are sensible and pragmatic. But this behavior is not functional during transition. It has more to do with hiding than with logic. It is denial and fear disguised as hard sense.

The resourcefulness and craftiness of the forces of resistance are sobering to contemplate. Even the most effective change agents are masters of these arts. But if this is disheartening, there is good news as well. History is full of people and organizations who broke through this barrier and created genuine, life-affirming transitions. And we know how they did it.

## Reading the Philosopher's Road Map

During eras of great change, when the old paradigm and its culture are impaired, we are able as never before to look more critically at the world, to see with new eyes the practices that guided those who created breakthroughs when life was difficult.

One of the great treasures our ancestors held was a rich tradition of myth that engaged people deeply, offering direction during times of upheaval. The greatest of these myths have survived because the truths they tell span the ages. They work no matter what the circumstances are.

Among the most enduring is the legend of Parzival, a popular medieval hero whose story was told by many writers, including a Bavarian knight named Wolfram von Eschenbach. Wolfram's version of this myth, written in about 1200, at a moment in history when the foundations of life were in confusing flux, speaks intimately to us about our own lives and times.

The legend of Parzival can be used as a guide, read as if it were a road map. It is not an ordinary map, but a philosopher's map that provides a profound description of the territory of transition. This map aids us in locating compelling goals and shows us roads that lead to them. It helps us determine when we have come to a crossroads and opens our eyes to the choices at hand. It identifies the traps we are most likely to encounter along the way and points out how to handle them. It identifies possibilities and how to seize them, and provides us with measuring devices so that we can see where we are at any given time. A philosopher's map is the change agent's most valuable tool.

This map is always deeper and more revealing than the one we are given by the prevailing culture. That other map makes assumptions: your career will define who you are; if you are hard working and talented you will overcome the obstacles that are in your way; because of the victories won over these forces you will march directly from success to success; and eventually you will arrive in a land where gratification, respect, and safety live.

The problem with this map is that it is false. It leads people astray and then leaves them stranded. Life does not work this way. The crucial obstacles we face are not external. Careers do not define people and career paths are seldom marked by a victorious march to success. Nor is there a land where gratification, respect, and safety live. When this map's failure becomes clear to us, we are frightened, confused, and, ultimately, paralyzed.

The philosopher's map depicted in stories such as the legend of Parzival is strikingly different. Its topography is realistic and honest and it may be used as a guide to practical action. Wolfram's description of his story makes it clear that this is a map of the unrestrained realities that make up real life. He wrote, "The tale never loses heart, but flees and pursues, turns tail and wheels to the attack and doles out blame and praise." Look now at some of the highlights of Wolfram's poetic tale. Read them as if they were key points on a map that has the power to transform the way you live your life as well as your ability to create significant changes in the world. See what discoveries you can make.

The subject of this legend is the search for the Holy Grail, a vessel of inexhaustible vitality, the source of all knowledge, and the great healing device in the world. Even in the face of fear and uncertainty, it regenerates belief and confidence.

The Grail king who guards this revered object is not easy to reach. He lives in a castle deep in a dark forest and finding him is a great challenge. To make matters worse, the king, like most leaders during transitional times, is a failure. He inherited the job and does not know what he is supposed to do. As time goes by and life changes, he stays the same, but he spends a lot of time pretending that everything is all right, faking it, and dithering. Dressed in his fabulous armor, he rides for hours on his great horse, fighting, posturing, hurting, and getting hurt for no particular reason.

One day the king encounters a pagan knight, and, rushing into battle, he kills the enemy, but it costs him dearly. He is desexed in the battle and is left with a lance head in the wound that he cannot remove. He cannot live fully this way, but he cannot die either. Clearly he is not an appropriate guardian for the Grail; he is the very symbol of the inability to regenerate, to produce new value. His kingdom, says Wolfram, has become a wasteland. The economy is shot, conflict abounds, people are frightened and demoralized. In the wasteland people are inauthentic and afraid to think for themselves.

Among the practical powers of a myth is that it encourages us to solve problems by identifying with each of its characters. When we look at the situation from this multiple perspective, we cannot help noticing that there are many players in the story, just as there are many qualities in our own makeup. In this myth, and in life, we can change roles if we want. For a while we can do the work of another character who is positioned more advantageously. We can even play the part of the hero. So having used the king to help us understand how serious the impediments to action are during transitions, we can use Parzival to help us decide what to do about it.

As with heroes everywhere, Parzival starts out frightened, ignorant, and on his own. He knows that finding the Grail, which will transform the wasteland, means going on a difficult and poorly defined journey. He has been told that success will come only to a knight who is motivated by a spirit of unflinching love, enduring loyalty, and spontaneous compassion. This is an imposing set of qualities because it is not what he does that counts, it is who he is. He will have to become a new man in order to reach his goal. Most aspiring heroes return their gear at this point and go back to dithering.

The only way to succeed in this journey, says Wolfram, is to start out and discover your own best road. And the only guide is one that tells you how to remain undaunted and alert, able to make discoveries for yourself. So Parzival, our hero, the hero in us, starts out overwhelmed, not sure what to do and lost in a dark forest. For years he tries everything he knows to find the Grail castle, just as we struggle for years to discover how to live meaningful lives. When that fails, he tries harder only to fail again. As he thinks it over, he lays the horse's reins on its neck, and the horse, that noble agent of nature, ambles along in his own way and discovers the castle.

What Parzival learned on his journey is the model for us today in our efforts to negotiate the treacheries of transition. We may be able to succeed as Parzival did if we understand the lessons of his story, if we learn to read the road map. The lessons are many:

• Get started. A goal is reached not by listening to accumulated wisdoms, not by going off and thinking about it, but by actively living life and by plunging into the forest where it is darkest. Confusion and uncertainty are good starting points. In fact, it is impossible to understand the magnitude of the task in advance, let alone the appropriate responses to it. Only when you relax into it will nature guide you to the answer.

• Compassion is your greatest strength. Although Parzival did not know it, his job was to confront the Grail king and utter, "What ails you?" When he did this, the king would be healed, the wasteland made productive, and he would be given the Grail. We must ask the same question. We need to ask it of ourselves, those we live and work with, and those who lead us. And this question must be animated by a spirit of compassion, not criticism.

• You will not ask the right questions the first time around. Parzival didn't. He was too polite. He had been taught that a good knight does not admit not knowing the answers, does not ask embarrassing questions. His fear of seeming foolish inhibited the expression of his compassion, so when he saw the wounded Grail king, he kept silent and his mission failed. The king was not healed and everybody was disappointed. Parzival looked like a lousy knight and he left the castle in despair. He blamed himself.

• No matter what you do, you will suffer a series of humiliating defeats. Parzival rode back into the forest downcast and wandered in confusion for years. He made lots of blunders, and he was laughed at and vilified constantly.

• The ultimate goal will be reached only after you have discovered who you are. Parzival does battle with a pagan knight one day and before anyone is hurt, they discover that they are half brothers. For the first time in his life, a lot of confusing things begin to make sense. When Parzival discovers this other part of himself and identifies his full nature this way, accepting himself as he truly is, a messenger appears in the forest glade and leads him to the castle.

• You do not need to find the answer to all your problems. You only have to ask the right question. This is great news, although of course you won't ask the question until you are awake, engaged, and compassionate. When Parzival discovered himself, he reached that point, so this time when he sees the wounded king he is unable to hold back his compassion. He asks the king what ails him without even thinking about it, and the healing occurs. Nature has a way of healing herself. Our job is to ask the questions that align us with this process.

This is a map we can follow. Its depiction of the journey rings true. It tells us what events to anticipate, urges us to expect breakdowns and also breakthroughs, and tells us the secret to success. That secret is inside us and it is powerful. It has to do with compassion, perseverance, and trust. This same map has served people for thousands of years; the complex knowledge it contains has guided masters of change in every historical era. Even though it presents an account of the basic human journey through life, when we study it closely, we can see that it is also a remarkably personal, utterly unique map. This philosopher's road map shows us a journey that has never been seen on this earth before and one that will never be seen again. It is the journey to discover our own potential.

Knowing that this map exists is the first step in creating breakthroughs during transitional times. Learning how to use it is the second.

# 2

## Dialogue

A philosopher's road map is a vital tool for change agents, but it is complex and difficult to decipher. Learning how to get value from this asset comes from engaging in a deep and active dialogue with life.

The way we communicate reveals how we experience life, how we can be expected to act, and how others should respond to us. Communicating effectively is the key to self-knowledge and to generating transitions, but learning how to do it is more than a matter of technique. It is the acquiring of a deep understanding of our thoughts and feelings, and of how we relate to other people.

Because this is so vital and evokes such strong feelings of self-protection, we spend most of our communication time hiding, obscuring, and misleading. We create false paths, roadblocks, and traps for those who would genuinely know what we are about. And the person we most often fool is ourselves.

At work this means that we can be expected to react in canned, nonspontaneous ways to everything that happens. We will respond to new information as if it were the same old song, get into predictable conflicts, be rigid and positioned, even if this way of doing things does not work well for us.

Effective communication, on the other hand, starts before the talking begins. It is two-thirds listening. It involves listening to ourselves, to other people, and to the world we live in. Of these three, listening to ourselves is the most difficult and is the key to success with the other two.

In order to communicate clearly and with conviction, in order to connect and have an impact, we need to have a good sense of what we actually have to say. For most people this is a rare occurrence. It means moving through the warning voices that chatter in our heads, that tell us to be careful, not to trust our perceptions, not to reveal too much. Past the judgments we habitually make about our shortcomings and others' inability to understand. Past the need to be right about how the world is and how we are. Beyond the public character we act out with so much energy every day and night. It is beyond these gatekeepers that our deepest, most unique thoughts lie. When communication comes from this territory, we feel that we are saying and doing things that truly matter and others tend to notice and respond— they feel a bond.

Yet if we want to speak from a place deeper than these surface voices, we must first give the voices some respect. They need to be moved through, not rejected. We created them painfully and with care. It took years and great effort to construct them. When we were young and largely defenseless, they saved our lives, or so it seems. If we feel that the voices have begun to hold us back, that they often lead to procrastination, to abrasiveness, to feelings of anger or helplessness, or to other sensations that make life difficult (and they do), dealing with them begins with respecting them.

More than two thousand years ago, the Chinese military strategist Sun Tzu wrote that the foundation for winning any battle begins with overcoming our own destructive inner conflicts. The first step in this strategy is respecting and understanding, not hating, what we want to change about ourselves. We must not underestimate this inner opponent, he notes, for it can be as powerful as the part of ourselves that desires change, and it has been around a long time building strength and learning to survive. The behavior we do not like is a natural part of ourselves; it is aware of the same weaknesses and draws on the same strengths the rest of us does.

In employing this strategy to discover what we really think and feel, we are not attempting to destroy the part of ourself that wants to confuse matters. Instead, we are using its strengths in a new way, working to refocus our energy and to restructure our way of responding to life. This may sound difficult and it is, but people do it every day. And it is worth the trouble. During the moments when we are on this road, we are less afraid, have more energy, and our vision is clearer. We feel less inadequate, victimized, and angry. We are less threatened by our secret beasts, by people and events that habitually tyrannize us, by unexpected or unexplained phenomena. At work we can see what is happening in the organization and in the marketplace more clearly. Listening to ourselves with care and affection can lead to the communication of thoughts and feelings that are genuine, on target, and interesting.

Accepting what we discover when we listen to ourselves leads us to listen to others. People who do this are more likely to form relationships that get mutually rewarding results. They less often make agreements that are not kept, or that invite sabotage or inaction. Mutual listening predisposes people to do what they have agreed to because they have been responded to on a deep level and their personal gratification comes to rest on successfully tackling jointly determined tasks.

The process of listening to ourselves and others takes time, but in the long run it takes less time than misstarts, disagreements, excuses, and smoldering resentments do. In the short run, breaking this addiction to the mood-altering fantasies we regularly entertain about ourselves is hard work that requires guidance.

I know a number of people who do this well. They are adept at moving other people into action and at generating agreements that produce effective results. They have a simple rule for communicating effectively: everything begins with a relationship.

Before uttering a word, these people honestly explore their goals, feelings, and intentions and know the desired result of the conversation. This is less common than you may think; to see someone in action who begins from this basis is often startling. Then they must work to discover what the other person is willing to hear. Although the conversation will go beyond that, this is not where it should start. Because coaches have specific results in mind, they must create an understanding that will lead to action.

Then they focus on the other person and the possibilities that matter to him or her, only talking about something that matters to themselves when there is an opening. If someone obviously does not want to hear something, they do not say it until the foundation has been built. That does not mean that they run around trying to please people. What it means is that if they want to get something done, they look for what is possible and do not waste time being impressed by the sound of their own voices.

The conversation should be an invitation to the other person to explore his or her motives, feelings, and intentions, and then to take action. It is not uncommon for people who are involved in this procedure to find themselves acting with purpose and dispatch to achieve goals that they genuinely care about that had previously seemed impossible. They are often delighted and surprised. They recognize that they only get their way when other people get theirs, so they listen very carefully to themselves, to the other person, and to the environment. Anyone who can do this will move mountains. It is an essential practice for anyone interested in changing the way people work together.

## Philosophy as a Guide to Action

To become an effective change agent, to bring about a transition that realigns an organization with its environment, is to come out of hiding and to learn how to communicate authentically with the world. It is a practice that is not taught in most schools and organizations, but it is an ancient art that can be revived.

This is not the first time in the course of human affairs that people have been confronted on a large scale by personal relationships that tend to be blocked, by institutions that are unable to deliver what they promise, and by leaders who have a difficult time compelling belief. This is the theme song of human life, and throughout history it has been the task of every generation to come to grips with it.

We are always somewhat in hiding because any culture changes more slowly than people's emerging needs do. Our concepts of who we are and how we should behave lag behind our real needs, and it is difficult to accept our feelings or to be acknowledged fully for being who we are. If you think this is a modern problem or your own secret sorrow, consider the fact that Aeschylus wrote "Zeus unlawfully rules with new laws" several thousand years before *Future Shock* was published.

As time passes the old values and beliefs that once so compellingly called to our deepest feelings and urges, summoning us to action based on a genuinely felt connection between ourselves and the world, begin to seem like stories. We explain everything in a businesslike manner devoid of direct human meaning, and great parts of our intellectual and emotional makeup are seen as inappropriate vehicles for grasping the meaning of life and for taking serious action.

This has been the case in the modern world for generations. Seminal sociologist Max Weber early in this century wrote compellingly about this dilemma. "The fate of our times," Weber said, "is that man must dwell in the disenchantment of the world." The result of this is a despair and cynicism that isolates and paralyzes us. This, said Weber, is a common response to life in the modern world, and he urged us not to succumb to it.

But how do we do this? How do we move through our defenses to discover what we feel and think, and what we want to create? And having done that, how do we learn which parts of our freshly evoked dreams to pursue with abandon and which to modify and negotiate about so that others will join with us to create something that is broad based and enduring?

Finding a guide for this activity is difficult. But it is there. The guide is philosophy.

That word puts many people off, but it doesn't need to. Engaging in philosophy is not something that requires an advanced degree; nor is it an activity that involves reading obscure books and listening to self-important teachers. It is personal and spontaneous. It is a daily process of inquiry into our thoughts, urges, feelings, and responses to life. It asks the deep questions that elicit truths about ourselves and the world.

Without some form of philosophy we are dragged through the streets by the emotions, conflicts, and problems that comprise daily life. We can be overwhelmed, and convinced that we are helpless and without choices. But philosophy has the power to modify this because it can guide us to use daily activities as a process of discovering who we really are, what we really care about, and what we can contribute to the world. It can be more personal, more interesting, more moving than anything else in our lives. It can put us in touch with our human roots, our deepest stirrings. Through philosophy we come to know ourselves as the authentic beings we are.

Some of this work can be done alone. The function of philosophy is to help us remember, to *remember* what we know, what we care about, who we truly are. It is personal and speaks from the heart. But it is social as well. It is a dialogue and tradition that cannot live in isolation. The good life of the individual, according to Plato, is inseparable from the good life of the community.

To succeed at this work we need strong partners and teachers with whom we can exchange questions and observations. In describing how to do philosophy, Plato uses Socrates as his model teacher who asks probing and often unsettling questions. Socrates makes it clear that our real lives, not some abstract musings, are the subject matter of philosophy. If we listen carefully to his teachings, our lives will never be the same. But taking Socrates as our teacher does not mean we are going to be told what to do or how to think. It means to enter into a lively dialogue where we question, probe, challenge, and learn to trust our responses to life. It is our own truth we are seeking, not the truth of someone else.

Because it is a basic understanding of Greek philosophy that the guidance we seek will come through our own spirits and minds, when a student encounters a great teacher, he or she is not abashed at the teacher's wisdom; the student's own wisdom emerges and grows in response. And then both teacher and student recall what they naturally know about life. This can be a strong foundation for action.

Philosophy is an especially appropriate guide to action during times of transition because it does not rely on the beliefs of a

culture that is no longer fully functional. Nor does it wholly reject those beliefs. It provides a process for new discovery and it
opens the door for seeing alternatives where none had appeared
to be.

Those who practice philosophy begin to pay genuine attention to themselves and to the world. They are able to measure
their thoughts, feelings, and intentions against the results that
the new environment generates. If they stay in dialogue with
themselves and with others, they become increasingly adept at
seeing what is there, rather than seeing what they want to or
what they have been told to see. The Socrates in our lives is deep
inside us and in those who will join with us in a probing and authentic dialogue of discovery.

## Applying Philosophy

People who come to know some of their hidden aspects will notice that they have choices about how to respond to the
challenges daily life presents, and that it is possible to become
less stuck and more at home in the world as it is. An example in
the workplace can be seen in the dramatic changes that can occur
when people are trusted, guided, and valued in a way they had
not been previously. Suddenly, on their own, they know what to
do about situations that had debilitated them. So powerful is this
force that even a small dose of it may have a significant impact.

Helen has been a waitress for well over twenty years and
she is tired. She has troubles at work and troubles at home.
Sometimes she is pleasant to customers, but not often.
When she snaps at someone, they snap back. When she
provides outstanding service, something that happens less

often all the time, it is taken for granted. Her work world is made up of more unpleasant exchanges than she would like, but she is used to it and has come to feel that this is the way life has to be. At times she is almost overwhelmed by despair.

Then, several years after a quality-assurance program was begun, she was named runner up in the Employee of the Month Program because of her efficiency. She did not win; she came in second and that was enough. This acknowledgment slipped right through her anger and defensiveness, and it touched her deeply.

A week later, still glowing, she said, "When they announced my name, I thought 'No, not this old broad!' I was shocked."

"Most of the time I don't like my job, but it has saved my life more than once," she continued. "When I think there's no reason to go on, something like this happens and I realize how much this job means to me and how much I enjoy most of the people I wait on. It keeps me going."

When Helen is acknowledged, she snaps out of her daily rut. She remembers something powerful: what she cares about and who she is. She makes contact with her customers in a way that is gratifying to them both, and instead of being a source of despair, her work brings her joy.

Following her award she was effective and energized, and although it would have taken much more than this to make these discoveries a permanent part of her life, it was several weeks before she returned to being angry and tired most of the time. That's a big bang from a little notice.

Helen was experiencing one of the effects of philosophy, the process through which people acknowledge a deeper part of

themselves than they usually do. Doing philosophy means to
notice and acknowledge those moments when wonder, doubt,
or clarity appear. This recognition of a direct connection
between the forces inside us and those in nature is available to
everybody and it appears spontaneously, but we seldom acknowledge it.

Learning to listen carefully to ourselves, noticing what
moves us, what interests and frightens us, and discovering what
we love is a difficult process to master and it takes courage. In the
course of taking these repeated deep looks, we will often be
startled and occasionally distressed by what we see. But it is a
magnificent process, and its eventual impact is to kindle an eros,
or love, a compassion for ourselves and the world. As we locate
this eros inside ourselves, we locate a strong wish to come out of
hiding. We begin to realize that there is more to life than we had
acknowledged and we want to continue this process of discovery.
The discoveries we make this way begin to seem familiar. They
seem to be something we have known all along, something we
are just remembering. When we remember this way, we remember who we really are.

In the place of opinions, judgments, and fears about ourselves, we begin to see a more authentic, complex person. We are
less embarrassed and more able to communicate with others.
That communication is vital, because if this awakening is to be
sustained, it must happen in a dialogue with others and with the
natural world.

This was how Socrates lived daily, and his ability to be
himself is the core of what he has given us. Plato tells us that
Socrates described himself not as a philosopher but as a midwife,
and Plato sees others giving birth to themselves through the
regular process of Socratic inquiry. Being ourselves is the goal
of philosophy. And this self, throwing off the need for protec-

tion and isolation, experiencing the need to connect that comes with eros, is able to act effectively with other people in the real world.

## Taking Action

You probably have a limited interest in sitting around the office discussing philosophy or higher ideals, however. You may fear that other people will raise an eyebrow or make remarks that evoke barks of laughter at your expense if you take on the airs of a philosopher. And they will. But the process I am recommending invariably leads to action. Its goals include coming to know yourself better, becoming more effective, and forming relationships that will get things done that you cannot do yourself—relationships that will bring into the world something that did not exist before.

This journey of discovery and the daily reporting of the findings is energizing and leads to effective results: ideas that work because they are reality based, solutions to problems that grow out of understanding the real nature of things, concepts that make sense to people because you devised them unfettered by limiting beliefs.

Does this mean that if you master this practice, people will stop disagreeing with you, that you will be seen as wise and good? Definitely not. This dialogue leads to an acceptance of everybody's humanity, not to perfection. What it generates is a capacity to appreciate all the disagreements, to accept them as natural, and to learn from them. If your focus is self-knowledge, you will be so interested in finding out what you and others feel and think, how you respond and dream, what you can do and create, that you will become lighter, more focused, and spontaneous. Your interest in the perfidy of other people will diminish, and the common occurrences and mischances of life will not devastate you or block your ability to take action.

Beth was known as The Bitch. When she was in one of her moods, her glance had the power to wither. As if there were a force field around her office, people avoided her, warning each other not to cross her path. At these times she was domineering, opinionated, and not willing to discuss alternatives. She knew about this reputation and used it to get her way.

Tom was a department head who reported to her. She frightened and intimidated him. He felt he could not please her and he hid from her whenever possible. Tom was tormented by her judgments and her sarcasm, and he was not sleeping well. One evening when he grew short of breath, his wife thought he was having a heart attack and rushed him to a doctor. The doctor told him that the problem was stress, and asked what was bothering him. Tom told the doctor about Beth and the doctor said that the situation was not good for his health, and that he should do something about it. Tom went home discouraged, not knowing what he could do, convinced that nobody could reason with Beth, thinking that losing his job was not good for his health either. He felt trapped.

At this time Beth was working with my partner and me intensively and she occasionally frightened us, too. One day after she unloaded on us, my partner Cheryl said, "Beth, when you talk like that, it's impossible for me to feel close to you." "Good," said Beth, "when I talk like that I don't want you to feel close to me."

Cheryl persisted, telling her that this way of being might seem natural to her, but that it blocked her ability to be effective on the job and would not help her chances of career advancement. Beth said that she knew this. Cheryl asked Beth if she liked this state of affairs. Of course not, responded Beth, but what could she do? She too felt trapped. Cheryl asked if she wanted to work on it and Beth replied that she did.

Beth began to notice herself, looking for times when she overreacted to people, times when she became sarcastic or positioned. Occasionally she was able to modify her behavior. Sometimes she left the room or otherwise avoided trouble when she felt the urge to get someone; other times she did not notice or did not care and sailed into someone with gusto.

We were working with Tom, too. We told him that nothing would shift until he was able to stand up for himself, to signal that he was not willing to play the old game anymore. We coached him on speaking forcefully, clearly, and respectfully, suggesting that he tell her that when she spoke like that he felt upset and overwhelmed and that it made him angry. He agreed that this was a good idea, but doubted he would be able to blurt it out.

Then one day Beth encountered Tom in the hallway with some of the guys from his department and she lit into him. Demanding that he defend a decision he had made, she was sarcastic and loud. And for some reason Tom talked back. He told her what he had done and why, and added for good measure that he did not appreciate her tone.

This was the moment all of us had anticipated for months with hope and uncertainty. Without a pause, Beth said, "You're right. You didn't deserve that. I'm sorry. "

Next morning at her weekly staff meeting she told the other department heads about the encounter, said that she had a problem with this sort of behavior from time to time, and that they could support her by letting her know, as Tom had, when she was doing it. This was not a shamefaced, difficult admission for Beth; it was a moment of relief and exhilaration. She felt more powerful because she knew that she was not automatically the prey of reactions she did not understand and felt she could not control. Her staff listened with unusual intensity, with surprise and hope.

The more Beth and Tom looked at what they were up to, the better they worked together. Responding to her admissions and her new openness, he acknowledged hiding from her and occasionally being vague and secretive. When she played Bitch, he played Little Boy and sometimes, he began to realize, he ran and hid first, provoking her sarcasm.

She acknowledged hunting him down when she suspected him of being Little Boy. She told him that it triggered her anger and resentment when he did projects for the vice president without her knowledge, because it changed everyone's priorities and endangered the timely finishing of projects on which she had made commitments. Cheryl and I helped them devise a process of setting priorities and sticking to them, of checking back with one another periodically to monitor progress. And it worked.

Tom's medical symptoms disappeared; he spent more time on projects and less time fuming and hiding. And Beth began to enjoy working pleasantly with Tom and with others. People began to notice; they told her so and talked to each other about it. She loved the attention.

Two years later the agreement holds. There have been some close calls, but no disasters. At times Beth gives in and just blows somebody away. She has learned not to expect that she will go around being compliant and sunny all the time. But she is warm and pleasant, funny as hell, and effective more often now than she used to be, and she is developing a charismatic leadership style that surprises and delights her.

Beth knows that occasionally The Bitch will reappear, but she also knows that she has a choice, and very often she chooses to be effective. Tom's Little Boy character will surface from time to time too, but he feels that he has some say in determining when and how. Beth and Tom have a lot in common and they have come to know it.

You may feel that the designation of Beth as The Bitch is cruel. Beth certainly thought so. But in settings such as this, people will be cruel, and that is the reality she had to handle. It is a reality many women have to handle. At a time when women are gaining power in many organizations, this is a name that is often thrown at those who succeed. It is difficult for them to know when this word indicates that they need to modify their behavior and when it indicates that someone is being vicious. Men are also subjected to character assassination, of course. It is one of the painful impediments to honest and humane working relationships that those doing philosophy must look at honestly. But if taking the look is occasionally unpleasant, the results can be gratifying.

Beth and Tom were engaged in a dialogue that was able to generate deep and unexpected insights about themselves and the world that I have been describing, and the results were impressive. When they began to remember what they really cared about and who they were, they were able to reach beyond their fears and make a meaningful and pragmatic connection. Because they stayed in communication, both of them continued to grow and to like themselves more fully because of it.

This process of remembrance is the core of doing philosophy. But it is only part of the process that is necessary if people are going genuinely to free themselves and the organizations they work with from habitually dysfunctional relations.

## The Importance of a Philosophical Work Group

Philosophy cannot be practiced in isolation. It is developed and made useful only through participation in a group. Such a group has its foundation in the Socratic gathering of friends who engage in a dialogue that is designed to touch each participant deeply. This dialogue is a series of questions and answers that encourage participants to learn how they feel and to discern what they know. It strips away the confusions of daily life and puts them in touch with a part of their being that is unafraid, that thinks and feels without impediment.

An interest in moving beyond discussions of how bad things are brings these people together. An urge to break through their own limitations and to make a difference attracts them to one another. What they discover every time is that the resources they need, the necessary strength and knowledge it takes, already live in them and their colleagues. Together they summon up a great power and use it creatively.

Group members become adept at discovering the emerging laws of nature or a marketplace, or the patterns of social interaction inside an organization. They come to have a direct, authentic way of interacting that excites a broader understanding of new ideas and moves others to action. They keep individuals and institutions in touch with the times, and they fight inertia, cynicism, and fear.

A free movement of mind and spirit can be evoked in these groups that lifts people to acts of boldness and balance, brilliant insight, and original creation. This alert state of mind is the great product of transitional groups, from those that invented the high arts of civilization in ancient Mesopotamia to those who produced modern technology.

This sort of group is essential for transformative change, personally and organizationally, and it can be created by anyone. Its members need to agree that honest feedback, respect, and enjoyment will be its hallmarks, but it may appear in many forms. It can grow out of the activities of a work team, an executive committee, a brain trust or task force, a group of colleagues or friends. Its grounding in the search for self-knowledge, however, must be acknowledged and pursued with discipline and candor if it is going to lead to the state of mind that creates inventive and transformative results.

Ultimately, this dialogue permits people who share in it to agree on the nature of reality in a way that frees them from habits and beliefs that block genuine vision. When this way of being is uncovered, participants long to be in touch with life as it is, and with other people as they are. They are able to perceive, clarify, and interact in a way that is new, widely understandable, and occasionally profound.

I urge you to form one of these groups and respect the work you do there. The activities should be guided by a set of practices that will produce a high level of self-knowledge and intellectual probity. Although the practices can vary, a specific set of disciplined activities will be necessary if this group is going to avoid boredom, arrogance, or irrelevance. Part Two of this book identifies six such practices. Each is a method for staying alert and engaged. Each is a philosophical discipline designed to produce self-knowledge and to build the power a change agent needs to contribute significantly to organizational transformation.

These practices are meant to evoke your greatest strengths, to call forth your unique abilities. They teach how to respect yourself and others, how to cope with your own uncertainty and resistance, how to handle conflict, exhaustion, and fear. Through them you come to recognize a vision that genuinely moves you and develop an ability to seek it with integrity. They will steer you along the roads of the philosopher's map.

But even if you do not form a group, you should seek the same honest dialogue in the relationships you have now and in those you form as you go about doing this work.

# II

## Six Practices

# 3

## Discover Your Vision

Effective change agents must have a strong sense of where they are and how to move toward a meaningful goal. The maps of reality that come with the traditions of myth and philosophy are essential to this work. Myth provides assurance that this strange transitional territory is real and that you belong here; it brings recognition and clarity. But that is only the start. Once you know where you are, you must find a way to look honestly at this reality and respond to it. You need to know how to spring into effective action, move down the road, stay in motion, and negotiate the real-world obstacles you face. How do you do this?

You should begin by paying attention to your values. Discover a compelling vision that will serve as your fundamental drive and guide to action. As the word implies, vision is the expansion of your ability to see and acknowledge what is going on around you and in you. There is much to be seen in this territory; some of it will seem contradictory, but a genuine vision is so moving that it drives you to set goals, work with others, shift and become flexible when your efforts are not fruitful. Vision is practical.

It is also essential to transformation. It makes sense out of a wide range of ideas, perceptions, and feelings. As the vision becomes clear, factors that had seemed like random information, perhaps overwhelming or confusing, fall into a meaningful order. So eventually do goals, strategies, and priorities. What you do not want to do, or are not suited for, also becomes clear.

A vision is made up of deeply held feelings and thoughts that tell you what you truly value. It is what Plato referred to as remembering. And once you identify a vision that is truly compelling to you, you know more about who you are, what values you want to foster in the world, and what contribution you want to make to their creation and perpetuation.

Discovering your vision is not an easy or quick process, however. People who live and work in settings where personal and organizational visions are not present and honored tend to keep their visions hidden, even from themselves. They have learned to go about their work without the discipline that comes from this great force. In its absence, people engage in mind-altering activities, internally created drugs such as strident ambition, anger, and petulance, or that classic response to disconnected power structures, listless and ambivalent behavior.

Change agents who want to introduce the concept of vision to a workplace should not do it casually. The vision search is one step in the process of breaking out of the habitual way most of us have of doing our life and work. Interrupting these ingrained behaviors that obscure vision is like trying to stop an addiction cold turkey.

The vice president was a self-starter. Nobody had to tell him what to do or why it should be done. He had always worked hard, and he got great results. But now that he had risen nearly to the top, he began to feel that something was missing. After years of intense labor, he had come to feel that he had sacrificed his personal life to a job that was not gratifying, and he was tired all the time.

This is a man who got where he is by taking decisive action and taking it now, so after many months of contemplation, he made a decision. The company was not what he wanted it to be. It was not an exciting or satisfying place to work. He decided that he would pour his considerable energy and frustrations into restructuring the place from top to bottom.

"What really drives me crazy," he said, "is that things aren't done carefully in this company. We don't plan, we don't monitor results and pull together. I'm tired of being the only responsible person around here."

He set about to create an energized, hard-driving management team. He knew that this would be a major undertaking and that it would encounter entrenched resistance, but if the managers would not move on their own, he would move them into becoming a company that cared and one that got results. He met with his boss to discover his priorities. He suggested new goals and began helping him draw up strategies. He became the power behind the throne, developing plans to strengthen the workforce, actively supporting those who were contributing to the company and looking for weak spots as well. Reluctantly he recommended that a divisional manager be fired, that a department head be put on formal warning. He set the standard for cutting waste, driving on some business trips to save the company plane fare. He drove his staff to work harder. He drove his boss, and mostly, he drove himself.

He hoped his boss would get the big picture and begin to take action but slowly it became clear that it was not working. The boss did not change. He did not need to because the vice president was doing everything. And the organization did not change either. Following his decision to jump start the company, the people he worked with became more frightened rather than less, more addicted to mind-altering fantasies—fears, rigid positions, a my-needs-first focus—than they were before. This wasn't at all what he had in mind. He became more tired, frustrated, and isolated than ever. He was stuck.

In responding to his dilemma the vice president took action, but he did not slow down, take a breath, and listen to himself. When this happens, the result is often cruel. What seems to be a courageous new line of action turns out to be more of the old driven behavior. Without the shocking clarity that comes with genuine vision, people tend to repeat what has not been working. In trying to create change without looking for a deeper foundation than his frustrations, the vice president reinforced his own dysfunctions and those of the organization. This is devastating. It convinces people that they really are trapped and helpless and it represses vision and invention.

## The Visions of Leaders

There is no shortcut to creating deep changes. They will only be brought about by someone's vision, a vision strong enough to penetrate the layers of resistance that encircle every organization. A 1991 *Harvard Business Review* analysis of corporate innovation in America concluded that "the single biggest detriment to innovation isn't a lack of capital or talent or market opportunity. It's corporate self-deception. Almost without exception, at the root of [most of the failures] is an organization that's kidding itself about what it really wants."

At times such as this, it is a good idea to recall the old wisdom that nothing is so practical as a good theory. You need to pause to figure a few things out. Figure out that difficult abstraction: what do I genuinely value, what is my vision for realizing that value, and where am I now in relation to my vision. This is a crucial step for a leader. Only after this work has started will clear goals begin to emerge along with the focused strategies and messages that compel support from others.

Vision is an abstraction that lives at a deeper level than the habitual behaviors that tell us how people always do things, how we always do things, how life always turns out. It speaks to us passionately—without the fear of offending or being embarrassed—about what we love and care for. It circumvents the voices we all carry in our heads that tell us we do not deserve or could not handle success. It is deeper than our fears that if we succeed we will leave someone behind, deeper than the judgments that we and/or others are not up to the task.

In a business arena, vision breaks us away from an obsession with immediate results, with the bottom line for this quarter and all other varieties of short-term thinking. It develops our ability to see ahead and make long term plans, to invest in the future. After this capability is developed, there is plenty of time to ask the bottom-line questions. In my work with decision makers, I often use the following exercise to put them on the road to discovering their vision.

Everyone sits in a chair opposite someone else and one of them agrees to be partner A who will speak first. I assign partner A the task of pretending that it is three years from now, that he is sitting in a cafe and has just spotted an old friend who has been out of the country for the whole time. They tell their friends about the wonderful three years they have just had. Everything they could have hoped for has happened at work. All their goals have been met, goals they would not have dreamed of have emerged and come true. Life is great.

Partner B in this dyad plays the old friend and his or her job is to be a committed listener, to encourage partner A to tell the story with gusto, leaving no details out, always speaking in the present as if it were three years from today. When the first speaker has finished, the partners switch with partner B telling his or her story. At the end of that time, everyone who has been participating in the exercise tells what stood out, what was interesting or surprising.

The second round begins with everyone taking a new partner. They tell the story again, adding any new ideas that come to them or that they heard someone else say that they would like to incorporate. But they add a new part. They tell their partner what they overcame in order to achieve this goal.

There is a third and final round, this one too with a new partner. They tell their tale again, adding anything they want to, but they also tell their partner who they enrolled in the process, whose support they gained in order to succeed.

When the talking is finished, everyone writes the answers to the following questions: What parts of my story were especially compelling to me? What did I enjoy talking about most? What did I leave out or not enjoy? What did I realize needed to be overcome in order to succeed? Who did I need support from?

This exercise moves people spontaneously past their "rational" barriers, past some of the concerns in their work and personal lives that keep them from getting clear. It puts them in touch with their genuine dreams, with that territory where their greatest energy and abilities lie.

This is just a first step, of course. More work needs to be done to gain clarity on what parts of this vision can become goals, to develop strategies to realize the goals and determine if the organizational support is available. But without this deeper knowledge of what you value, your activities will be characterized by predictability and a lack of energy and focus.

The process of becoming fully acquainted with his or her vision may be the most important thing a leader can accomplish. In 1989 Warren Bennis studied more than thirty of America's most effective leaders. Taken from every field of activity, his leaders responded at length to questions on what drove them and what qualities made them effective. He concluded that the primary characteristic his leaders had in common was a "guiding purpose, an overarching vision."

This vision may be something you just know so that it is possible to move directly into action, but more often it is part of a longer process, the ongoing, lifelong activity of genuinely getting to know yourself. "At bottom," writes Bennis in *On Becoming a Leader*, "becoming a leader is synonymous with becoming yourself." Good change agents are leaders, regardless of their position in an organization. This research corroborates an ancient understanding about the nature of leadership. In the sixth century B.C., the Greek poet Pindar advised the ruler of Syracuse that to be a great leader means to "become what you really are."

## The Need for Vision-Based Strategies

Because genuine visions produce real-world results that are personally engaging, people are less likely to be sidetracked by the addictive urge to stumble into the trouble that characterizes superficial goals. Deeply held visions lead to strategies that are strong and alert, that contain calculations that take into account resistance, turmoil, abuse, and other activities that are a natural part of transition.

Change strategies that are not vision-based, on the other hand, tend to be timid or unclear, designed not to cause trouble. But major changes always cause trouble, and a strategy is an abstraction that tells you what trouble to cause and what trouble to avoid. Its purpose is to shift the balance of power, or to stop somebody else from doing that. If it works, it is trouble for somebody. But vision-based strategies evoke an alertness and perseverance from those who believe in them that help them avoid the destructive trouble that will impair the chances of success.

Vision tells you how to choose among other options as well. If it is made public, and it must be, it tells others what you intend, it brings hidden issues that might block movement out on the table before they can work their subterranean erosion. It encourages negotiation processes that elicit the support of coworkers, and greatly diminishes the chances of getting into the fray with colleagues who were running according to a different map than you are.

A strategy that grows out of a vision process can be built on new knowledge that emerges along the way: knowledge of everyone's strengths and how to deploy them, their weaknesses and how to compensate for them; knowledge of what you truly want as opposed to what you think you should want, and a realistic assessment of the organization's ability to carry out its strategy. At the heart of any successful strategy is an understanding of what is unique and valuable about an organization. And a vision, this deeper voice that is totally unique, will be the essence of its competitive advantage.

## Why Organizational Visions Are Rare

But genuine organizational visions that are powerful enough to drive strategies and to assure implementation are rare. I once asked a group of twelve CEOs if they had a mission or vision statement for their companies. Eleven of them did. Of those eleven, only three knew what it was. None of them reported that it made much difference to them. They had one because everyone else does, but they did not know why. They are like the sisters in Mozart's opera *Così fan tutte* who, when they hear someone speaking Latin, remark, "That may be true, but I don't understand it."

This is a vision statement without a vision, and it is more related to the problem we confront than it is to the solution. The vision I am speaking of is knowing what you love, what you care about, what you want to have happen. It is deep and compelling. It constantly develops and grows. So striking is this phenomenon that when you find the words that even approximate it, you are moved. You disengage automatic pilot.

On automatic pilot you do the same things over and over again, never seeing a way to break the cycle. A CEO recently told me that in the years he drove himself hardest, he would get frustrated that the results were seldom there and he would begin looking for the person who was making the mistakes, who was not measuring up. He would brood about it and occasionally he would call in employees and fire them. "I would see the confused, frightened look on their faces and it made me mad. Why hadn't they seen it coming? Why did they think they could get away with not performing? On those days I would leave the office fuming."

If addictions are behaviors we use to alter our moods in a destructive way, this overwork-and-blame syndrome has to be one of America's greatest addictions. While we are in the throes of this activity, we are driven but blind to what is really going on around us and inside us, we are busy but inefficient, and we are confused. We do not know what we care about or what we stand for and we don't know where we are going. Whatever we achieve is without a context and it is not satisfying. Nor do we know when we have reached the end, or when we can stop and enjoy ourselves and other people.

Because we do not identify this behavior as addictive, we do not see how dangerous it is, and unlike an addiction to drugs, this dependency seems on the surface to be adaptive and honorable. But like addictions to drugs, driving yourself blindly is very expensive. I know a company where the leaders grew increasingly distressed by the evidence that their market share was steadily decreasing over a six-year period. They decided that enough was enough, that they had to take action. Without stopping to look deeply at their position or their resources and constraints, without identifying a vision and new goals, they decided to renovate in order to outstrip the competition. Since time was of the essence, they got to work right away. They worked hard and they put in long hours. The result was that within two years they were completely renovated, gleaming, and new.

But business did not improve. They found themselves out of their old market but not in a new one. Their old clients left and the new ones they got could not pay the bills. Most distressingly, they did not know what to do about it. They did not know how to act natural in these high-class surroundings. They did not appear like the real thing to customers. They did not appear like the real thing to themselves, and they could not develop a strategy that energized them, their work force, and clients.

Surveying the wreckage several years later, the president identified the problem: "Without knowing who we were, we went out and spent ten million dollars." They still do not know who they are and they are still not making money, and the competitors they were obsessed with are also in bad shape.

Most people know that change strategies built on a foundation of fear or impulse rather than on vision and honest evaluation will lead to big trouble, or at least they suspect it. So when all the articles began to appear a few years ago saying everyone needed a vision, lots of people got one. Most of them bought one as quickly as possible so that it would not interfere with running the business. A great gush of statements about caring and quality and how everybody is a family sprang up. Leaders hoped that this would make things better. It did not. In many cases it made things worse.

> A medium-sized manufacturing company was not keeping up with the competition, and rather than look at their mission, their resources, and their abilities in relation to the marketplace, they mounted a major quality campaign designed to increase employee productivity. The corporate office started it off by creating a vision statement and asking every department to do the same. Then they sat back and waited for the transformation in the offices and in the shop, for the improved efficiency and increased sales. But after six months nothing seemed to change.
>
> The corporate leaders became disenchanted and angry. They looked for people who were not following the plan and as a result decided to fire the popular division manager. Employees were furious. They said it put the lie to their leaders' claim that they knew what had to be done and that they cared about the employees who would do it. A move that top management felt was a necessary response to a specific crisis and not in conflict with the quality campaign was seen as part of a tired old pattern by the rank and file.
>
> From the first the employees had viewed the vision and the quality program as a new way of packaging the old manipulations. And this firing confirmed their suspicions. "The old man is doing it again," said a long-time employee. "He fires the division manager every two or three years; been doing it ever since he took over. He brings someone

pretty good in for a while, gets scared that he is spending too much money, and brings in someone else who is supposed to cut costs and bleeds us dry. Whatever he says he's doing, it's just what he always does. He's been making stupid decisions for thirty years and if he lives long enough he'll make them for another thirty."

This sort of mistrust is common today. Quick visions are a convenience. They do not speak from the heart about matters that are so strongly felt by the people at the top that they are willing to change their own ways in order to achieve the vision. Leaders' messages saying they care are often followed by layoffs. Memos about the importance of quality coexist with evaluation systems that stress efficiency and ignore quality. Leaders who do this usually hope they have started a new chapter in employee relations but instead their actions often convey a message of "Fix yourself, I'm busy." Programs they hoped were instructional and motivating instead generate new expressions of employee cynicism.

## The Visions of Workers

Employees asked to write vision statements for their departments are often skeptical. They sense another manipulation, another experience of being told to pretend that their greatest dream is to do everything the boss wants while the boss continues doing business as usual.

As one meeting was about to begin, a woman asked if I knew or cared that this was her day off, that she had better things to do than sit in another meeting. She noted that she had heard about all the vision statements of other departments and that she had one, too. Hers was going to be a demand to be respected, to have a word in determining work conditions, and a request that she hear about her good work as well as her bad work.

This is a natural response to a sudden request that employees declare a vision. The mechanics of real change are never smooth or uniformly pleasant. In most cases, employees who do not respond this way are too frightened or depressed to speak up. I prefer the anger. It is usually genuine, appropriate, and it can be worked with. Authentic employee visions tend to come packaged with a set of requests that management change its way of interacting with them. This is a problem only if management gets rigid and huffy about it.

For leaders the constraints on knowing and realizing their visions are significant. They have considerable responsibility. They know that they must mobilize a whole organization, compete against smart competitors, and deal with a fickle economy. For most employees the barrier to knowing and articulating a genuine vision is simpler but more confining. They know that for the most part it does not matter what they think or imagine.

Employees who find themselves in this situation tend to feel that their power is not in their dreams but in what they refuse to do. Many are convinced that only if they cause trouble do they get their conditions improved. And this state of conflict is unlikely to shift unless a major crisis comes along that temporarily leads everyone to pull together, or unless top management is suddenly moved by a vision that is so compelling that they have to make their employees into genuine partners in order to pull off something extraordinary.

And most bosses know this. They are afraid to encourage sessions where employees say all those nasty things they have been saving up. They see this as a way of needlessly stirring people up (one manager said, "I feel like I am being sent a bill that I am not going to pay"). Yet it is simple to take the first step in moving toward a vision, even with angry employees.

> At a meeting of restaurant employees, Joyce—who was born to be annoyed—asked if I cared about the fact that these meetings were "bullshit." Her proof was that the new program had not resulted in employees being permitted to participate in making the decisions that mattered most to her. She hated the color they had painted the restaurant walls and none of the waitresses had been consulted. Her eyes flashed, her voice rose, and she was just getting started.
>
> Asked why, if she was so angry with management, she went out on the floor every day to wait tables, her answer was the typical and appropriate one. She needed the money. "Why earn it this particular way?" I asked.
>
> "Because, dammit, I love watching closely to see if I can pick up on what people want, I love to guess when they need help with a decision or when they want something more. I just love it when I can get something for somebody that they didn't know they could get, or when a regular customer knows they can count on me to remember what they like or what their allergies are."
>
> She was joined in a chorus by the other waitresses, describing their joy in this sort of activity, telling stories, laughing, and appreciating the exchange. And then they wrote their vision and Joyce led them. It was a beautiful vision and writing it gave them pleasure. They have told me since that when things got rough they liked to recall writing this statement.

Visions that are genuinely written by the people working in departments, and left in their own words, are great feedback for decision makers. They tell you how people feel about their work, the place they work in, and how they view themselves. If, at first, these visions reveal conflict and anger, they are a great diagnostic, providing detailed information on what needs to be done.

## Visions That End Relationships

For others, the discovery of a vision may lead to movement out of the organization. If a smoldering discontent has been building, the process of generating a department vision and work standards may bring employees to choice. They may feel that they do not want to work in a place that expects genuine results, they may decide to go do some other work that is more reflective of their real personal vision, or they may take the vision home and realize that their personal life is not gratifying and move to change that. Sometimes this becomes a genuine personal awakening.

When Jay went to work as a copywriter for a large corporation right out of graduate school, the first person he got to know was his boss's boss. Jane was a phenomenon. Brilliant, assured, witty and clever, she was also cultured, well paid, and dressed perfectly. She took Jay in hand and taught him how to dress, how to talk, how to read the corporate tea leaves, and she groomed him for better things. He loved it and was an excellent student, though he got a little testy when she tried to make him read Proust and stop watching trash on Sunday morning television.

Then one day Jane called Jay into her office for a frank discussion. She had seen his personnel file and could see that he was not on the fast track, so she suggested that he plan to go someplace where he would be appreciated. Her strategy for his career shift and his execution of it changed his life.

Think long and hard, she told him, about what you want out of life. Then go to the newspapers and professional journals and find the perfect job, one so wonderful that you know you are not ready for it yet. Then set out to market yourself for it. Do an inventory of your talents and professional skills, your personal attributes and dreams. Go to these people and tell them why it is right for you. Because you know that there will not be a chance in hell of success, you can afford to go all out without the fear of failure and embarrassment.

Jay did this. He found the perfect job, did the inventory, got an interview, performed like a champ, and they made an offer. Shocked, he called Jane and asked what he should do. "Tell them you'll take it if they give you a car," she replied. He did and today he is a big-shot executive with these people, and one of the most competent executives in St. Louis.

This was a vision-driven move. Jane's suggestion that Jay do a personal inventory and then apply it to the marketplace took him out of the habitual behavior that characterized his previous work and gave him a look at his deeper yearnings. And when Jay took the new job, this vision found a tangible outlet that evolved and grew over the years.

Once begun, the vision process is not easy to stop and, because it moves us beyond most of our fears and resistance, it may lead to unexpected results. Those results may profoundly alter the course of many lives.

Dennis had worked his way up from the legal office to become the president of a corporation. Several years after assuming the position, he was approached by the chairman of the board and asked to develop a ten-year plan.

Dennis was thorough. He made an in-depth analysis of the company's assets, its market position, its personnel, and its prospects. He discussed possibilities with the chairman, members of the executive committee, and a few trusted outsiders. It was immediately clear to him that the company was no longer in the business it had been in twenty years earlier, and that 70 percent of its profits came from new enterprises.

He began to develop plans to acknowledge this and take advantage of it, but every time he tried to set up a process that would shift people in the company into new activities, it became clear to him that great struggles lay in his future. He could only envisage unpleasantness and dislocation. He grew depressed and upset. Looking at his new plan, he was not sure he wanted all this trouble, was not sure he was the man for the job, did not know if he had the drive and confidence to do it. A shift began to occur in him.

He began to look at what genuinely moved him. He explored his values, took a look at how he was spending his life and began musing about the future. It became clear to him that he needed to understand his own values, know his own vision before he could honestly complete his project. So I worked with him on this personal vision. When he completed it, he was greatly moved and his priorities were clear. He needed to be somewhere else.

Telling the owner his decision was not pleasant, but it was wise. After a period of turmoil and accusations, followed by inducements to stay, they settled down to develop a strategy that would identify both of their visions for the company. Dennis was able to make recommendations that were unclouded by his unexplored resentments and urges to escape, and the owner was able to determine where he

wanted the company to go and who could help him
do it. Dennis's search for a vision had destroyed a lot of
unexplored assumptions, it ended a relationship, and
produced two functioning visions. He was never sorry
he found it.

Nothing is as powerful or enduring as a vision, but it needs
support and nurturing if it is going to live and make a difference.
Dennis learned that unexpectedly in his search. Discovering your
vision, the first practice of effective change agents, will be most
ably pursued if you and the members of your work group entertain specific questions that move you toward knowing what you
genuinely value. First ask yourself how you would like the world
to be, what values move you most deeply, and what are you willing to do to see them live? Then, in the light of those values, ask
the following questions:

• What do you want right now, for yourself and for the people you care about?

• Why do you want these things and how badly do you want
them?

• How do you want to spend your time, now and in the
future?

• What sort of work relationships do you need to develop if
your goals are going to be met?

• How will you handle the most pressing roadblocks that
you face now?

• What possibilities for the future excite you most?

Vision made conscious taps a person's courage, perseverance, resourcefulness, and engagement with the world. It is vast,
somewhat mysterious, and it can only be partly known, but
working to uncover it is a vitally important process of discovery
and movement. When you find yourself in a dark forest as
Parzival did, where conflicting claims on your time and emotions

make it difficult to know what to do next, locating this vision on the philosopher's map and taking a step or two toward it will open the way to a previously unimagined freedom and gratification. Doing this work in the company of others, which is the only way it works, leads to the birth of previously unimagined creations.

# 4

## Understand Your Intention

No matter how compelling your vision is, if you do not truly want to bring it to life, you won't. Your most creative strategies will founder if you do not honestly pursue them, and work relationships that are dominated by gesturing rather than engagement are never effective. Intention is everything.

Knowing your intention is the key to effective action. And the way you come to recognize your real intention is by monitoring your decisions. If a thorough exploration of your decisions makes it clear that your intention is not what you said it was, then you must revisit your goals and strategies and make adjustments.

A vision has the power to transform an individual's life and to alter the road an organization takes. But to have this effect it must sooner or later take the form of a decision. A decision turns a vision into something tangible. It generates actions, responses, and results. It starts a chain of events that has a motion and a logic of its own.

This vision and the decision that gives it form do not need to be grand. In fact, it is best if they are not. The type of decision that usually leads to the greatest results is the one to take the next step. It may mean deciding to have a conversation to clear the air with someone or determining what outcome you want from a meeting. Decisions of this sort, made regularly, will significantly alter the way you approach life. They bring an increased awareness of yourself in the world and make it possible to become clear about what you truly intend to have happen. They also clarify what you do not intend to do and teach you how to avoid the pretense that you have a passion for these matters.

In order to demonstrate the power of this practice, I often ask clients who are about to participate in a seminar or retreat to answer a few questions in advance: What is your purpose for attending this meeting? If this meeting were to be a great success, what would be true at the end of it? What will you need to do during the meeting in order to achieve your purpose for being here?

The answers are wonderful and varied, but the most common one is "My purpose in coming to this meeting is to obey my boss who says I have to." A good, honest answer and more significant than it seems. Most of us go through our day doing what our boss says we ought to do, or what we imagine he or she thinks we ought to do, or what our fears or appetites decree. The habit of unconsciously doing things because we think we have to will never entirely stop. But we can be aware of it, use it to advantage, and alter it at times.

The ability to create value at any time or place is essential for change agents. It makes no sense to wait for everything to be just right before moving into action; you have to be effective when events call for it. That may happen when you are in a bad mood, overwhelmed by work, or being forced to do things you do not want to do. So once the seminar begins, each participant reads aloud his or her answer to the first question—the purpose for attending. Then each of them turns this declaration into a decision: I am here today to achieve the following result. Finally I request the participants to make a commitment to do everything that is reasonably in their power to achieve their goals by the end of the session.

The result of this mechanism is that those involved naturally begin to notice more closely what is going on. They hear their own voices more vividly because something they care about has taken place in the room; they have a stake in the deliberations and in the outcome. They see what others say and do, and they understand more fully the effects of their actions on them. They begin to realize that their goal is going to require someone's support, and that if they want cooperation for the achievement of this goal, they must assist others in reaching theirs.

Sometimes they discover that their goal was inappropriate, not possible, not daring enough, or off target, and they are able to change it. They do this by announcing their new decision so that others may work with them toward its achievement, or block it or ignore it. They become acutely aware of what works, what aggravates, what toes they don't want to tread on. For the length of the seminar they are more deft than they usually are. This process is enlivening. It keeps them playing hard and learning things they never expected to learn.

## Decisions That Evoke Strong Values

Forming decisions this way will also change your relationship to results. Unless you consciously decide what you want, you are only able to respond to any stimulus after it happens. You are reacting to already formed forces and events. There is nothing to connect you to results except your habits, judgments, and addictive reactions. Whatever the stimulus, your response is predictable and determined by factors such as fear and a desire to protect yourself.

The most effective people tend to be those who enter into a project enthusiastically, in touch with their positive vision. But this possibility is closed to those who are inclined to respond rather than initiate. If you decide in advance and become watchful and aware, you are not taken off guard. The event may be surprising, but you are armed with the knowledge of how you want everything to turn out, with an active awareness of your values and what contribution you want to make. And, oddly enough, if the event does not turn out as you had wanted, it does not sting as much. You know what has happened because you have been paying attention and you know that you have played fully. You tend to see more accurately why it did not work, so that next time you may change your goal or seek it more wisely.

In this territory you are conscious of being directly connected to the world. You learn who you are and what your values are, what works and what does not work. You come to know your abilities and understand your true intentions. Nothing is more valuable to a change agent.

Seminar participants are usually pleasantly surprised by the way they show up under these circumstances. It is common for them to articulate deeply held visions and compelling goals and to demonstrate an ability to reach out and connect with others. Moreover, they discover that it is more relaxing to be alert and in touch than it is to hide from events and the feelings they arouse.

Following this revelation, participants review their activities during the past week, noting when they were active and what the results were, noting when they were reactive and the results. They are invited to list the events that triggered their reactive responses and to determine what pattern they can see to it: what words or actions frightened them, what made them angry or caught them by surprise. They are asked to view any discovery they might make about these patterns as good news, a new tool to use to extricate themselves from the cycle of repeated drubbings at the hands of their own judgments and fears.

Then they are invited to think about the upcoming week and to make a decision about the major events that it has in store. They write the decision down and review it at week's end, looking again for patterns. This helps them see themselves a little bit as others do, learning how to handle situations that trigger their urge to act unconsciously. This cluster of activities and questions is always eye-opening, and it is a good mechanism for you and your work group to use as you work on the second practice.

## Why Decisions Are Hard to Make

Some decisions are difficult to make because they are a direct challenge to the powerful forces that keep you from taking effective action. One of these forces is internal, and it comes from the needs to satisfy appetites: the needs to eat, drink, have sex, be accepted, and similar drives. Another force is socialized needs. They are the slavish engagement with the values you grew up with, ideas about who you are and who you should be, of what life should be like and how people should treat you. A third set of needs has to do with your judgments, with notions about your limitations and fears, wild surmises about the shortcomings and motives of those around you.

These factors weigh heavily on everyone I have ever known. Religions have been built and philosophies constructed to help us cope with them. Escaping from them is not done easily. It does not happen as the result of a weekend workshop, time-management skills, an MBA, or a quality-assurance program. It does not happen because someone tells us just to say no. It will not happen because you have read this book.

When you are in the grips of this force, you drift along taking life as it comes. Often upset, swearing to do better, you are life's victim. Determined to stop smoking or drinking, to diet or exercise, to be more organized or to stop being frightened by people at work, you still do not change. Life seems predictable and it is. Even if you are successful, you are not gratified.

If you are a change agent, sooner or later you must confront this force, choosing to live more openly, alive to your surroundings and the stirrings inside you. This means deciding to escape the stranglehold of daily events and fears, deciding to live with intention. Only then can you help the organization you care about to do the same.

Understanding your genuine intention and making the decisions necessary to bring it into being means beginning the day by deciding what you want to do and what you want to have happen. This action requires that you take time to think and feel about what accomplishments would gratify you. It means that you will do more than rush headlong into the day's activities, letting events fall as they will and reacting to life's depredations.

It suggests a solitude where you probe your mind and spirit. And if you do this well, you will probe with a sense of care and interest, solicitude and affection, rather than with a sense of duty and foreboding or anticipatory blame. You will advance into the day with an understanding of what work you want to accomplish, what joy you want to give or receive, and what you want to know. You will also come to understand the limits to this activity and learn to let up on yourself and those around you when it is best.

There is a story that demonstrates both the power and limitations of decisions of this sort. It says a lot about how one person's intention affects another person's intention. It demonstrates how a new context can be generated by a few decisions, a context that clarifies goals and the rules of the game, and it demonstrates how you can work contentedly with someone you may not like.

In many organizations people are saddled with nicknames that are intended to hurt. Lois, the powerful director of advertising at an office-supply company, was called the Ice Queen behind her back. She knew what people said about her and claimed that it did not bother her, but I think it hurt like hell and drove her further into isolation.

Her employees told us that she was cold, disapproving, and unresponsive to their needs. When they asked her how to do a task, she told them the question meant that they were lacking in motivation, otherwise they would have found out how to do this work on their own. She acted as if errors were made on purpose, yet she was upset to discover mistakes that could have been avoided if people had only come to her for advice. She said that good work was rare, and that when it occurred, it did not need to be acknowledged because that was what people were hired to do.

She was a hard-working woman who stayed late almost every night and came in on weekends. She felt that those who chose to go home on time were not interested in getting the job done, and she looked down on those who seemed not to match her commitment.

Although this attitude did not make her popular, to many on her staff she was a secret gift from heaven. Most of them had been working at the place for years, and their jobs had been relatively easy. Records were not kept carefully, marketing strategies were not based on research, good ideas and timely reports were yearned for but not required by management. But a new management team had begun to change all that. They wanted market research and they wanted useful reports. So her accusing, aloof manner was catnip to her frightened and outraged staff. Here, clearly, was the reason for their unhappiness and inability to perform according to the new standards that were being applied so suddenly. Their anger was prodigious.

The angriest, or at least the most vocal, was Marge. She felt used and did not care who knew it. She said that Lois, while unpleasant to everyone, had it in especially for her. She told of unfair assignments, greater workloads than those of her colleagues, vicious remarks, and threats to fire her. When asked about this situation, Lois simply said that Marge might be able to do her work accurately and efficiently if she did not waste everyone's time with her complaints.

Then one day Lois said she wanted me to come to her department to improve working conditions. I asked if she realized that her management methods would come under scrutiny in the course of this work and, looking at me firmly, she said that she understood.

This project was launched with enthusiasm and some progress was made. There were meetings where complaints were grudgingly given up in the interest of developing recommendations, negotiations where Lois agreed to change some important rules, and a war of attrition where both sides tried to change without giving up being right. This is basically regulation. After several months they could see some improvement in communication and they had developed some mutual goals. But the context was still warlike, the goals were muddy, and they were all ready to embrace failure so that they could lay the blame at someone else's feet.

This sort of breakdown is difficult but natural. It means that a start has been made, that people have gotten down to basics—down to questions of what do you value? who do you trust? what do you want to create? and how badly do you want it? This is necessary to making a problematic relationship shift so that it can grow more healthy. But this stage is a good one only if it is acknowledged and responded to immediately. So I made an aggressive recommendation. Do unto Lois, I said piously, as you would have her do unto you.

Snorts of derision and stunned disbelief greeted this recommendation. Some employees were furious; others expressed pity. Apparently I didn't understand, said Marge, that Lois is oppressive. If we treat her nicely after all we've been through, she will feel vindicated and strike out at us. The Ice Queen will sting us bad.

Bring her out of isolation, I told them. Take responsibility for your half of the relationship. Get together as a group and decide to take on an activity or project. Let her know about it, then do it. I told them that I would return in a week to see if they would undertake a project.

Then I met with Lois and pressed her in a similar fashion. In her work with me she had identified her department's strengths and weaknesses, and the advantages and problems in her way of working with her staff. It had been easy to develop a frank and open relationship with her. So just as I had urged her staff to treat her as they would like to be treated, I made a proposal to her. "What would it feel like," I asked, "if you were to thank your employees when they did a good job?"

"I don't know," responded the honest Lois. "I've never done that. I imagine it would feel false. I think they'd suspect that I was put up to it, and they wouldn't believe it. They might make fun of me behind my back."

She told me that she had come to believe in firm discipline years ago when she was growing up in a large family with few resources. They had succeeded in life only because of her mother's strength of character and determination. She told me some moving stories about it. The efforts to change Lois's interactions with her staff must have seemed ineffectual and weak compared to this stirring model of a mother's courage. It was difficult to imagine Lois's mother patting anyone on the head and complimenting his or her work when there was more to be done, more discipline to be summoned.

"One of these days," I told her with a persistence Lois's mother would have appreciated, "you will find yourself thanking your staff for doing a good job. It will feel great. It will make a difference in your ability to be understood by them and to evoke higher work standards." Lois was skeptical.

And then, more quickly than anticipated, the staff took action. They did not wait for my return to plan it. The quarterly marketing report was due the next week, and management's new work demands were more than the department was configured to handle. The usual ritual was that Lois came in all weekend to finish up, grumbling about her feckless staff, feeling lonely and ill-used. This month, however, the staff told her that they would like to stay late Friday evening in order to finish the report. If they all kept at it, they might finish that evening and Lois could have a free weekend. Lois thought it might work. She let them try it.

They got right to work, went at it enthusiastically, and by ten o'clock on Friday night, excited and proud, they had completed the task. Lois was amazed. And before she knew what she was doing, she thanked them. It just slipped out.

She thanked them again. And then again. (Once you start thanking people, it can be difficult to stop.) They all ended up laughing with her. It was heady stuff.

After this event Lois was able to see more clearly. Her goal, previously muddied by anger directed at her staff, became easy to articulate. She wanted to retrain her department to do the work that was being required by management. She wanted them to have the tools and the support to get the job done. Their success was essential to hers, and she knew what to do about it. Her actions were no longer blocked by secret hopes that they would crash and burn so that she could be right about what flunkies they were.

She decided to have a staff meeting every week. She saw to it that the staff got proper training, she got new computers for everyone, and occasionally she took them out to dinner. At first her staff had difficulty trusting this new regime. But the genuine spirit that informed the meetings, the new openness and expressiveness, the computers, and the training began to bring down the barricades. They were getting to be pals.

These changes were not made quickly or easily. They took many months. A lot of effort, a number of carefully overlooked remarks, and some rebuilding of broken alliances were required. Lois was often frightened by her own openness, and her staff was frightened by the new work standards. But little by little the department was rebuilt. The decision made by the employees to help, and Lois's decision to allow it and to thank them, decisions to take significant risks, bore their fruit. By the end of three months, this department had transformed itself.

Both Lois and her staff had made decisions to move beyond some considerable and well-founded fears and to act in the interests of making life more constructive and pleasant. This was a beginning, an opportunity for building a new set of expectations and standards, constructing new ways of communicating and developing a new culture that would be strong over time. The people in Lois's department became a reference group for each other and for her. The members of a reference group pay attention to one another, becoming models for how to respond to events. Over time, they teach one another to break away from old habits and beliefs and to come forward with new values and ways of acting that can influence the outcomes of crises, projects, and opportunities. Reference groups are the most powerful force in shifting intention that I have ever seen. This one was truly impressive.

And then, three months and one day after the process had begun, Lois fired Marge. Not very nicely, either. She called her in, said that she was doing a horrible job, and told her to pick up her last check. Marge did not leave quietly.

This, too, is instructive. It points out the limits of dramatic change. Culture may shift, behavior may change, but who we are and the forces that drive us to contention do not suddenly end. There are always surprises, unexpected advances, and shocking reversions during this process. These are not factors that are amenable to control; they are events we can learn from. Through them we may come genuinely to know our intentions; we may not like them but we can learn to live fully in them and create value with them.

Although it may be tempting to be annoyed with the Loises we encounter, this temptation should be resisted. Those of us who do not know what courage it takes to give up trying to change other people and instead to shift our own way of being are poorly positioned to become lofty about other peoples' limitations.

Change agents who look for magically new people or actions to result from the work of a few months are fools, and fools in trouble if they promise to produce them. And effective new results can be had short of this utopia. In fact, the most realistic results often come from the tension of people moving between the worlds of action and contemplation, of their Ice Queen sides and their partnership capacities. To fail to undertake a problem for fear that unpleasant characteristics will emerge, or to try to make them go away by creating rules that limit topics of discussion to those that seem safe, is to engage in anticipatory surrender. And it only postpones the trouble to a time that you did not choose, when it may emerge explosively.

## The Folly of Combat

The decisions made by Lois and her department freed them from long-term combat. Once this has happened people have a shared experience to guide them to a new way of working out problems. They can look at the pattern of their interaction and, without resorting to the never-ending task of determining who is wrong, they can learn what activities trigger retribution.

People who are willing to do this can see the harm that is generated when they are in the grips of the need to have their colleague be wrong so that they can be right—and ineffective. And they can learn to say, "Here is what I do when I am upset or frightened. Here is how you can call me off." In this way the focus remains on the goal, and judgments are stripped of their power to divert attention from the task at hand and to cripple effective action.

Karl and Betty had worked together for years. Each knew
the other's tricks by heart. Although their working relationship was often good, when push came to shove and
there were scarce resources to get hold of, they always
declared immediate war. A deadly but quick struggle took
place with the result that both of them and their departments suffered.

A big event was coming up and an out-of-town executive would be there. It was one of life's great pleasures for
this man to find a glaring error or two, and he was not
bashful about making his displeasure known when he did.
Fear was in the air. Karl ran around like the good soldier he
is, doing *this* himself, doing *that* himself, handling every
detail he could. Overwhelmed. Betty planned meticulously
and in advance. She knew what her resources were and how
to deploy them. No stone was left unturned, nothing was
out of place.

But hours before the event, a key employee of Betty's
called in sick. Betty got a replacement who happened to
be one of Karl's backup people. Soon afterward, Karl discovered that he needed an extra hand, so he called the
same man only to discover that Betty had locked up his
services. Karl slammed down the phone and steamed out
of his office to find Betty. When one of her spies told
her Karl was coming, she started as if a bugle had summoned her.

Karl and Betty advanced on one another in full armor,
flags flying, and met in armed combat in the hallway. By-
standers sang of this battle for months.

Both of them knew why this had happened. Karl knew
that Betty's imperious manner would never let her admit
that she should not raid other people's troops whenever she

damn well wanted to. Betty knew that once again Karl's lack of organization was taking him down. They told each other these things and threw in a few other choice remarks as well. Some terrible wounds were sustained, but neither of them gave way. Nobody won.

Finally they both spun around and headed back to their offices. A second replacement was eventually found, but both Karl and Betty were tight-lipped and short of breath during the big event. Those who had witnessed the battle, or had heard about it, tiptoed carefully around the combatants for days. They were afraid that doing what one of them asked would offend the other. Life was more complex than it needed to be.

Although this was not their worst battle, it became a triggering event. Having had enough, approximately nine years of it, they were able to establish a new process with the help of a facilitator. He worked with them to identify what triggered their anger, and then what they were willing to do to come off it. They got specific and detailed about the triggers and what feelings they had as a result. The facilitator suggested that when these feelings began to steal over them, they could let the other know how they felt and then choose to move toward the successful achievement of the goal and away from an obsession with being right. Looking at the painful results of fixing on the other's bad habits, they found it possible to focus on the goals rather than the anger. They practiced it, learning to clear the air, but not with the expectation that the other would change his or her method of working or develop a new personality structure because of it. Eventually they discovered their own way to call a truce when combat threatened.

Today Karl remains the good, overwhelmed soldier, and Betty is still convinced that all resources are hers. But they know how to extricate themselves from the traumas these roles generate. They are willing to let the other be infuriatingly human and they are able to get on with the task at hand and not tie their stomachs in knots every time a big event comes along. Now, more often than was previously the case, they show up as the competent professionals they are. And it is a lot more fun being around them.

This is a case where two old soldiers were able to take a good look at what they were up to. They saw that their intention to be right was stronger than their intention to get the job done. Once identified, the havoc wrecked by this state of affairs was clear to them both. This knowledge and a lot of hard work produced a shift in work habits. They became ongoing partners in a process of discovering how to break free of enticements to go to battle.

## The Song of the Sirens

In order for this process to work, the parties must come together and acknowledge that something is not working, that life does not have to go on like this. They need to focus on their own dysfunctional behavior and acknowledge it, actually embrace and accept it. The knowledge of how to work in this way has been around for thousands of years. My partner Sam Taylor describes one of the roots of this understanding when he is working with clients. It comes from the myth of Odysseus and the Sirens.

Because he has provoked a heavenly displeasure, Odysseus is having a miserable time trying to get home to Ithaca after the

Trojan War. Being a hero was not enough to assure him the support of the gods. Killing off bad people and being decent and honorable in the face of hardships were not enough either. A small error annoyed one of the gods who decreed that his life must be a trial. (You may be able to identify with this.)

At the point our story begins, his ship is about to sail by the island where the Sirens live. These spirits sing beautiful songs that enrapture passersby. But every sailor who is lured to the shore to hear the song is dashed repeatedly against the rocks and dies a horrible death. Fortunately a nymph has taken a liking to Odysseus and she—an early consultant—advises him wisely. If you want to hear the song, she suggests, fill your sailors' ears with beeswax and have them lash you to the mast. As you pass the island, you will beg them to free you so that you may head for shore. Instruct them to pay no attention until the island with its danger has passed. He followed her advice and eventually got home safely.

The Sirens' songs echo through the ages; they sing in our ears constantly. Betty and Karl were listening to them when they did combat in the hall. Lois and her staff were well acquainted with their music, too. Every judgment we make about ourselves and others is a fragment of this song. Although it promises wisdom and knowledge of the future, it takes us off course and leads to destruction every time.

But philosophical work groups can provide the necessary protection for each of their members when these songs are in the air. Not wasting time condemning the Sirens or lamenting the urge to listen to their music, these groups can tie their partners to the mast—if the partner requests it—until the danger is over. Each one of them can know that they are listening to the song, and knowing it announce the fact. They can ask not to be listened to while they are gripped by this music, and they can tell their partners when the spell has passed.

## When Judgments Kill Off Change

The story of the Sirens contains vital information for those who want to participate in changing organizations. It is a beautiful example of the relevance of mythology to daily life.

The myth makes a new context available. Not the context of work or family where we are too close to the action, too concerned with the outcome to be really sensible, it tells us about a fictional character's actions and results. Because it is a myth, we are more likely to admire the hero who learns to avoid destruction at the hands of false voices and judgments and less likely to get defensive than we would if our own behavior were the subject.

Comparing our actions to those of the hero, we can better understand our intentions. His are clear. He wants things to work out right. Odysseus wants to get home again. We, on the other hand, are real people, and our intentions are more complex. If we are honest with ourselves, this comparison will show us that we are often committed to struggling, getting hurt, and being right. To hell with the goal.

These feelings, which are common and normal, have been with us all our lives. In the great majority of families everyone comes to play a rigid role designed to keep the family going. Our role becomes very important to us. We develop a strong attachment to it, playing this role so intensely and so often that we eventually come to assume that this limited way of acting is the only way we can be.

Some powerful needs are created by this situation. One is the feeling that we must be in control of our interactions, feelings, and behavior at all times. We feel frightened and ashamed to fail in this. Another is perfectionism, the need to be right. We develop a tendency to identify what might go wrong and to base our activities on avoiding that, rather than striving to achieve a positive vision. A third is blame, which is what we do when control fails, as it always does. We blame ourselves, the people around us, we even blame the dog.

Coming into the workplace, which is a new family, we encounter the same dynamics and we understand it immediately. So we act out our personal drama, playing our favorite role and assigning familiar roles to others, usually without telling them they have passed the audition. This pattern breeds in us a tendency to feel isolated and alone because our characters and the characters we make up for others are not whole or flexible. They cannot make contact with events or other people in a real, unpredictable world. Things do not go very well in this play; the outcome is always the same. Following each performance, we become objects of our own contempt, and we are hectored by a sense of emptiness.

A work culture that constantly measures our performance according to shifting and unknowable standards reinforces this tendency to turn our eyes inward, scrutinizing every detail of our feelings and activities and finding ourselves lacking. Feeling ashamed this way is both painful and paralyzing. This dynamic teaches us to isolate ourselves, and as a consequence we lose the benefit of healthy human feedback. Our vision is narrowed, our ability to think and reason is impaired, our response time becomes sluggish, and we cannot see alternatives.

Learning to ignore the voices that we use so harshly against ourselves and others requires constant vigilance. It is difficult to give full attention to anything else when they speak. This is not a good way to work and it is not a good way to live. But these judgments do not survive long in the light, so in order to recover from this we must come out of hiding and isolation. We must seek relationships where an agreement has been made, first to acknowledge the naturalness of these emotions and then to move beyond them.

Taking this step is a decision. It is the decision that Lois made, and the one her department chose. It was Karl and Betty's as well. But this decision would not have done them any good if they had stopped at noticing that their judgments made them difficult to work with. That would have increased their sense of shame, amplified the voices' power. It was this acknowledgment in combination with acceptance of the fact that this is natural human behavior, the makeup of heroes as well as everyday people, that produced the positive results. The results lasted because the acceptance was coupled with an agreement to follow a process that circumvented these judgments again and again. And they practiced this process daily.

The workplace is a wonderful arena for this process because it imposes some of the natural boundaries a myth does. Behavior there has specific goals, and the methods of measuring how well you are doing are clearer. This clarity can compel you to come out of hiding, just as Parzival left the darkness of the forest, and to begin moving beyond the voices that hold you back. It weakens the debilitating fascination with secret judgments and leads you toward the external world.

Learning the difference between limiting conversations about the world and genuine work goals can transform an organization as well. This knowledge may be used to construct a work setting with humane rules of behavior, one that acknowledges the Sirens' songs but speaks to the needs to identify with others, to belong and to produce results that serve everyone. These too are basic and powerful needs. So powerful that they can weaken an attachment to the perpetuation of secret monsters.

If knowing what you value is the first practice necessary for generating change, understanding your intention is the second.

In order to shift the behavior of people in an organization, you will need to live this discovery, teach it, and model it. Being conscious of what you are truly up to adds greatly to your compassion for those from whom you expect great changes. It is humbling.

# 5

## Work with Integrity

Organizations do not function well when honesty and responsibility atrophy, particularly at the top. People whose job is to change organizations or make them more effective complain about this all the time.

> The quality-assurance director of a large corporation pointed to the company vision statement mounted on the wall behind the desk. "That's a joke," he said. "People here are told to put these things on the wall of their offices. But everybody laughs at them."
>
> Asked why, he responded, "Nothing the company does has anything to do with that statement. Not a thing. And then, there is the origin. They stole it from another company. That vision statement is just p.r. And it makes my work more difficult because everybody knows that the big guys don't really mean what they say when it comes to caring about employees or being a family."

These complaints are far from trivial. We are approaching a crisis in organizational life today. It is rare for organizations to deliver what they promise. Leaders who are willing to be held accountable are hard to find, and people who trust their leaders are scarce. Yet legitimacy and genuine authority are necessary if individuals and organizations are going to thrive.

If you want to create a significant change in this condition, having the people in power actively on your side is very important. But this is so rare that change agents need to start out by assuming that leaders, even those who say they want to see deep changes, will not offer real support for these efforts. In a situation where change is vital, you cannot afford to wait for that to happen. Assume that you must build the power to effect change yourself. It can be done.

Nobody can give you the power to succeed at creating major changes anyway. The sort of power that arises during transitions is generated through action. Communicating honestly and responsibly is a form of action that creates this power. It invites honest feedback that allows those who practice it to discover what is going on with greater accuracy, to respond more quickly and to communicate effectively. This state of affairs is rare and compelling. It attracts people and it shifts coalitions. It is revolutionary.

No wonder honesty and responsibility are both longed for and feared. It is not surprising that those who practice them get attention, much of it negative. But these qualities are the key to producing deep changes. So, despite the risk, it is essential to work with integrity: to communicate honestly and responsibly.

In talking about honesty and responsibility, I am not speaking of that internal violence that makes people feel they should weigh every utterance to see that word and deed coincide. It is not always wise to speak only what is honest. There are times when deep feelings and thoughts are irrelevant or will unnecessarily hurt someone. There are times when secrets have to be kept. But if you find yourself looking for reasons to withhold ideas and feelings, if you are surrounded by secrets, take some time to explore the situation. Every less-than-honest exchange creates problems down the road, and the longer the concealment continues, the greater the problems will be when they eventually emerge.

This third practice begins with the assumption that honesty and responsibility are not a form of perfection, but attainable human qualities. Although they are difficult to define or to act out, people can move closer to them if they work at it. Developing these qualities is a discipline, a daily practice. One that is never completed.

Every time I tell clients this, I rediscover how frightening the word *honesty* is. They are afraid that I am going to tell them to blurt out the awful truth about their colleagues and bosses. They are afraid that if they say what they have been holding in all this time, they will engender anger, resentment, and revenge. They are right. Blurting out the awful truth is dangerous. Mark Twain recognized this when he said, "Truth is the most valuable thing we have, let us economize." By urging people to speak honesty I do not mean that you should indulge in a blast of pent-up hostility. That sort of talk is the kiss of death for a change agent. If, in the name of honesty, responsibility, or integrity, you go around announcing other people's flaws, you are probably not going to get much done.

## Why Nice Guys Finish Last

Successful change agents become adept at recognizing when their thoughts and feelings need to be communicated and when they do not. They also know that when change and turmoil are in the air, to hold in feelings regularly is not honest, nor does it produce successful working relationships. It certainly does not generate the power to create deep changes. Professional nice guys usually finish last, and they know they will.

To repress expressing how you feel about something can produce serious anger. This is an energy that nice guys have in buckets and are afraid to vent. They are beset by internal turmoil and it takes most of their energy to keep this force of nature bound in. So most nice guys take refuge in manipulation, the indirect expression of their feelings, wishes, and intentions. They keep secrets and do their work covertly. They are capable of appalling things at times. People tend not to trust them, although they often like them. "Ed is such a nice guy," they say, "I can't understand why he did that."

These nice guys run protection rackets. They create a territory around themselves where everyone is protecting and defending. There is precious little energy left for the forthright observation of what is happening in a fast-changing world, for the location of a vision, the creation of goals or the pursuit of them. A nice guy's strength lies not in taking action but in the covert manipulation of other people. But this is a phantom strength because manipulated outcomes are always precarious.

Withheld feelings are also tumultuous. They find their way to the surface at the most embarrassing times. When you are tired, under stress, or caught off guard, they come blasting out nastily. What you say at these times sounds out of context to people and your behavior seems out of character. And then, nice guys or gals who have blurted it all out usually retreat into embarrassment or isolation for some time afterward. They are not much good if there is a job to get done. Moreover, they often engage in elaborate and destructive ruses to create pity for themselves when they feel that they are in danger.

The senior vice president of a toy company was meeting with the executive committee from a regional center. He had deep concerns about the way the section head was handling his job. Revenues were down, there were cost overruns that did not make sense, and the executive team was not as creative or fast moving as he wanted them to be. This two-day meeting was designed to identify the problems and determine a strategy for dealing with them.

The vice president began the first day by reading a list of concerns and complaints. He took the section head to task directly and at length. By lunchtime, everybody was thoroughly frightened. The afternoon session was conducted in hushed tones, as one department head after another presented facts, figures, and other defenses listlessly and disconnectedly. They looked to the section head for guidance, but he sat there consumed by rage. They hoped he would step forward and lead them out of the quagmire on the second day.

As the second day dawned and he finally spoke up, it was clear that no leadership was forthcoming. "I believe in criticism in private and praise in public. I believe in being nice to people," he said. "This attack is unwarranted and upsetting. It's unfair and I can't even begin to respond to it."

The reaction was dramatic. Every one of his colleagues rushed to defend him. They made statements of support and directed angry remarks at the vice president and at corporate leaders. There was good reason for the anger and accusations. Unenlightened corporate policy had a great deal to do with the problems being discussed and the vice president's style had been offensive. But the nice-guy defense had not served the section head or his division. The day was wasted. No agreements on the nature of the problems or possible solutions were arrived at, no probing assessments were made. No mutual understandings were reached.

Everyone left the meeting angry and self-righteous. The vice president felt isolated from the executive committee and in the months that followed no remedial activity came out of the corporation or the division. The vice president never learned a thing about what he had done that was ineffective, nor did the section head. Results continued not to be there. Within a year the section head and several of his lieutenants were fired.

As was the case here, nice guys often do their stuff because they are provoked. Life and senior vice presidents have a way of not playing fair. Going into this nice-guy-gets-beat-up-for-no-reason act takes the heat off temporarily and enrolls others in the drama. It says, "I feel victimized and unable to cope." It also says, "If you buy my victim story, I'll buy yours." It often works. The oppression is usually real enough, and the temptation to give in to helplessness is great. But this is a far cry from an honest expression of fear or anger followed by the resolution to press forward. When people buy each other's stories, they are immobilized and incapable of taking action. Nice guys not only finish last, but they also take their friends down with them.

## The Dangers of Subtlety

Nice guys often think they are being tactful. They are dishonest in the name of decency. But being overly subtle is not a wise practice. It lets you pretend that you have made your point when you have not. You go away from a conversation telling yourself that you have been clear at last, and later when the results you wanted do not occur, you get angry. The other person, meanwhile, gets to understand the conversation any way he or she wants to and to choose pretty much any response at all. The question of properly understood consequences has not been raised. Confusion and hurt feelings reign.

Marcel Proust in *Remembrance of Things Past* tells the story of his two aunts who were homebodies and not used to conversing with outsiders. They developed their own idiosyncratic way of talking that only they fully understood. This form of conversation struck them as wonderfully civilized and they prided themselves on their subtlety. One day a neighbor who had recently given them a gift was coming to dinner, and the aunts were reminded to thank him. In the course of the meal, they each did so, quite prettily they thought. But the guest did not know what they were saying. He wondered why they kept making such odd remarks. He left not knowing that he had been thanked. And when the relatives turned on the aunts later, chastising them for their failure to thank their benefactor, the aunts were hurt.

Overly polite communication—not to be confused with simple human decency, which is always a good idea—is an agreement to take no action. If you are powerful, it is a technique you may use to make sure that nothing changes. If you need to create something new, it is the kiss of death. The overly polite always need a third party to move things into action. The seventeenth-century writer Mme. de Sévigné wrote that the two politest people to frequent the court of Louis XIV were so subtle that they needed an interpreter when they spoke.

The overly polite live in a world of inaction where what matters is nuance, gossip, and opinion. Every day their conversations take them further from their genuine feelings and goals. When this pattern is established, an unspoken and dishonest agreement has taken people to a place from which it is not easy to return. False sentiment is entrapment.

## Building Honest Boundaries

The practice of communicating honestly and responsibly, however, can alter that pattern. The declaration of a boundary is a way of recalling yourself from some interpersonal fiction that is getting you in trouble. It is a cure for many organizational maladies, but it is difficult to do.

Thelma had been a fabulous clerk: hard working, punctual, accurate, agreeable. Before long she was promoted to assistant manager, where she continued to excel. And then a reshuffling created an opening at the top of her department, and she was made department head. She was petrified. Now she had to schedule people, train them, and, worst of all, discipline them. She was a pleasant and compliant soul and this was torture to her. In fact, she had no idea how to do it. In her personal life as well as her professional life, she was largely without boundaries.

A classic pattern quickly emerged. If an employee did not like the schedule she had made out, he or she would complain and Thelma would change it. This usually created trouble, made someone else come in at an awkward time, or Thelma had to cover the shift herself (her husband hated it when this happened and there was trouble at home). She ignored problems between employees if she could and she ignored interdepartmental conflicts; she avoided her boss when he was in a bad mood, even if his advice was needed, and she was slow to promote employees for fear of making a mistake. Then it would get to be too much for her and she would fly into a rage. The people in her department never knew what to expect. They found it difficult to know which standards were real and which were not. They were often frustrated, disorganized, and ineffective.

They did not think this had anything to do with Thelma. She was usually so nice, made so many sacrifices for them. They blamed themselves, each other, and the company for the problems. Even when some of them quit, they said that Thelma was the only good thing about the department.

Nice as she is, people always act a little disoriented around Thelma.

Thelma needed to create boundaries, to know when to say no, when to set limits, and when to be flexible. Establishing boundaries takes practice and support. It means to be clear on what needs to be done, what your role is, and what you can do now. It does not mean that you have to learn to be strong or forceful all the time. All your fears and confusions can and will remain alive and kicking, but they can come to reside on the personal side of your boundaries most of the time.

Knowing your boundaries also means to begin speaking honestly about the matter at hand and taking personal responsibility for your actions. Understanding what honesty and responsibility mean in action is the best way to begin building boundaries.

## Honesty Revealed at Last

We know that communicating honestly is not founded on making personal judgments about the correlations between your words and deeds. It is not blurting out the awful truth about how wrong and doomed everyone is. It is not withholding feelings or being obscure. What is it then?

It is a simple thing. It means communicating in a way that cuts through the confusion and establishes what is real for you. It starts with understanding your own feelings, which are the filter you use to interpret what is happening in the world. It means saying to someone, "When you do that [or say that] here is how I feel."

That feeling is something about which you are the expert; it is your truth and not an assertion that the other person is wrong, has bad intentions, or a flawed character. It is the opening gambit in a dialogue—the other person *will* respond—that, properly constructed, leads to an easier, less complex, and more effective work relationship. And most crucially, it is the sort of communication that sets a new context, takes you away from the obsession with who is right and who is wrong, who is angry and who is hurt, who is dangerous and who can be ignored, and it moves you into an entirely new territory where there are two operant questions: What are we trying to get done here? What is the best way to go about it?

## Mastering the Art of Feedback

When I urge clients to talk like that, they blanch. Even timid people find a voice. Not a chance, they say, I cannot do that. I *will not* do that. Especially to the boss. I would not either; it is dangerous. To do this without having set a new context so that it may be understood is foolish. Most people have a limited interest in our deepest feelings, especially when these feelings take the form of criticism. And they know what to do when they hear it. Bosses are especially adept at this.

So the context must be set carefully. It starts with an agreement that people will work together more effectively if they know how they are coming across. They can only know this if they ask for feedback, which tells them what effect they are having. Feedback is not criticism or praise or encouragement. It is a mirror. It is as nearly neutral as human communication can be.

Feedback at its most useful relates you to the rest of the world; it suggests a connection between what you say and do and your results. It implies that if you are getting results you do not like, you can do something differently and get different results. This is not objectivity, or science. It is a way of noticing that has less of the emotional charge than most activities do. Because it is less emotional, it has a better chance of being heard and of generating new results.

It is the most useful tool I know of to create a versatile style of communicating, and it is essential for learning to communicate honestly. I recommend it whenever a group of people needs to change their way of working together in order to be more effective, harmonious, or creative.

Pat was not popular with her coworkers. They said she had an attitude. She was defensive, and she often seemed to be trying to see how many of the regulations she could ignore. She was loud at times and could speak coarsely. She was rude to new people in the department and got into lots of arguments with coworkers. Several people in her department said that they had considered quitting because she was so hard to get along with.

Pat could also be charming, open, and naturally amiable. She was bright and, when conditions were right, she was highly competent. I liked her a lot; I suspected that a number of her coworkers also did and that they wanted to get along better with her. For her part, Pat was fully aware of the situation, and although she put on a show of not caring, she was obviously hurt by it.

As her department staff undertook the task of writing work standards, I urged them to practice giving one another honest feedback. Carefully setting the context, and establishing rules for how to communicate honestly without being offensive, I asked them to write down what was working between them and what was not and to keep it to themselves. Following that, they were urged to propose some rules of conduct that might alter the situation and to announce them to the group. That was easy for them, but like Proust's aunts, they were indirect and overly subtle.

This way of talking, of course, seldom communicates effectively to those for whom it is intended. In this case, several of the suggested new standards, clearly aimed at Pat, were taken personally by Mark who was miffed and hurt. And Pat, who felt snuck up on, pretended to think they did not apply to her.

The next stage was to request that anyone who had feedback for another person in the room deliver it. They were requested to say, "When you do or say that, this is how I feel." They were not to say such things as, "You always . . ." or "Everyone here thinks that you . . ." or even "Perhaps you need help with . . ." They were asked to keep it limited to observed, specific behavior and their personal reaction to it. People are rarely willing to talk this way at first and they did not this time. Even those who were burning my ears in private with complaints about Pat lost their voices in the group.

Approximately three weeks after we started this procedure, however, Pat's closest work partner, Steve, took her aside and said, "Pat, when you don't finish your reports on time, it makes more work for me and I get angry with you." Pat, of course, had been waiting for someone to blast her, and when this feedback was delivered, she was surprised at how mild it was and how easy it would be to respond. This was information that she could receive without being indignant. Steve might not be so angry if she changed some of her habits.

She did change them and Steve was exhilarated. He felt powerful and was relieved of so much anger that he began to suspect that it had come from someplace deeper than his relations with Pat. He got to enjoying his time with her, felt a little conspiratorial around her, as if they shared a secret. She was a reminder to him that it might be possible to shift the nature of other relationships by communicating in this way.

Pat too was delighted. Here she was having a very pleasant time at work with Steve and it eased a lot of her fears. At the next staff meeting she announced, "I'm so relieved. I thought Steve didn't like me, but he was just mad."

This sort of communication does not come easily in the beginning, and people's reticence must be respected. The voice will be found only when the right time emerges; if pushed, this process can lead to unpleasant results. This process is not designed to "fix" obnoxious people; it is a method for creating a new group context, a new and accepted way of communicating. Only when this is understood does this sort of feedback have useful results. It is one step in a long process of opening up, generating newly shared goals, work standards, and trouble-shooting techniques. Eventually it may become part of a new culture where people are freed from some of the unnecessary difficulties that accompany unconscious communication patterns.

Properly constructed feedback invites people to bring hidden behavior out into the open, to acknowledge it in the safe confines of a group that will not embarrass them. It is the first hurdle in creating a mechanism that substitutes new activities for those that are causing unhappiness. People's boundaries must be respected when they are doing this. The discovery of what does not work, for example, must be done in a positive context. Negative feedback opens up great problems and it is destructive. Careful follow-up is always appropriate during this process.

On the other hand, it is a mistake to avoid this work in order not to awaken deep emotions. The everyday course of events in the workplace constantly evokes them, but without the support or knowledge that are part of a well-planned intervention. It is possible for people to deny for years that they are responsible for their own behavior, but when a supportive group sets strong standards, most people will respond. It is one thing for the boss to tell you that you are not doing your job well, and quite another when it comes from coworkers. Most people will change their behavior when this happens. Some will quit and go someplace where these expectations are not applicable. Others will hedge their bets, modifying what they do until the time when everybody forgets the new standards and it seems not to matter anymore.

It is important to remember that the behavior that upsets members of the group may be perfectly fine behavior. It may be marching to a different and more talented drummer; it may be behavior that is occasioned by experiences that are nobody's damned business. It is fine not to like the feedback, but it is crucial to notice what works and what does not.

## Breaking the Conspiracy of Silence

Honesty in this context, then, is a matter of communicating certain feelings publicly. It means the creation of a culture that breaks the conspiracy of silence—the way we have of pretending not to know the obvious, the way we have of expending enormous energy and lots of time protecting some secret or other. In seminars I often use a procedure to shift this activity. After participants have stated their reasons for attending, after they have made public decisions to achieve certain goals by the end of the seminar, and after they have gotten to know one another in this context and to trust me, I ask them to rate their participation so far. "How effectively have you pursued the goal you stated at the outset?" I ask them. "If you have really gone for it, rate yourself a ten and write it down on a piece of paper. If you haven't really tried at all, rate yourself a one."

Then they list every other participant in the room on the paper and rate them according to the same scale. They are not rating the other peoples' intelligence or diligence. They are not saying whether they like these people or their ideas. They are not commenting on their commitment, since nobody can know how much anyone else is committed to anything.

They are simply giving their impression of how effectively the person in question is pursuing his or her announced objective. They are saying to the person, I do not know what is going on inside you, but my feeling is that you are going for it at a level ten or eight or whatever. It is feedback. It can be vital information to someone who is not used to noticing how he or she comes across.

Then it proceeds as follows. The first person reads his or her personal ratings. Then everyone else reads their rating of the first person, who then can see how his or her evaluation matches up against those of others. Everyone in the room takes a turn; it is an eye-opening exercise. And it produces a sort of camaraderie, a feeling that everyone has lived through an experience of honest communication, has come through not only unscathed, but stronger, less afraid to hear what everybody has always known. And because it is well monitored, nobody has blurted out some awful judgment that will come back to haunt them. I have never seen a person who was not positively affected by this procedure.

Used on the job or in your work group, this way of giving and receiving feedback makes it easier for people to identify what they do that is effective and what is not. They are more likely to look at it in this setting because it is no longer an awful personal secret, but rather part of a public process where all sorts of behaviors are identified without being judged.

## Seeking Responsibility

If the word honesty frightens people, responsibility is a word that worries them. Asked to say what they feel responsible for, my clients will list their health, their jobs, their children, their parents, the death of a loved one, whales, snails, the Irish Potato Famine. The list is never-ending. I am often sorry I asked.

Responsibility conjures up a sense of duty, guilt, burden, and, occasionally, credit for what turns out well. To most people it means expecting themselves to control outcomes. This, of course, is impossible and seen this way, responsibility is something to be avoided. It is such an insidious expectation that people naturally flee from it. This cluster of feelings is not conducive to taking effective action. So we need a definition of responsibility that is human oriented, that is sensible and within the realm of possibility, one that induces people to seek responsibility rather than to fear it.

Accordingly responsibility can be defined as knowing what is happening and responding as best you can. The first part of that definition means practicing honest inquiry, looking at events in order to discover what you can of the truth. It means that you have an interest in what is really happening that is greater than your interest in being right, greater than your interest in not knowing or in having things seem to be what you want them to be.

Doing this is to come out of hiding where you are always weak, ashamed, and limited in your ability to respond. Through the honest expression of your feelings, or the assertion of a goal, you clear away part of the energy that blocks vision and movement. Yet if you do only this, you will be forever emoting. It is great to stand center stage and sing your aria occasionally, but if you do not move from that into action you lose peoples' goodwill.

The next step, then, is to look again at the decision that got you started. Look at the goal or objective that moved you to take this job, undertake this project, engage in this relationship. Is your original decision still good? Do you want to alter it or make a new one? Become reasonably clear on that and take responsibility for moving toward it.

To do that, use the clarity that comes to those who have unburdened themselves of a secret sorrow in order to look honestly at the reality they confront. Ask questions: How do I define my goal now? How near the goal am I? What assets do I have in the struggle to reach it? What liabilities? What external factors will influence the outcome? What trends can I see? What am I really up to here? What is working? What is missing?

These questions can be answered with remarkable accuracy by listening to your thoughts and feelings, the thoughts and feelings that tend to lie just below the fears and obsessions that so often distract us.

Properly understood, responsibility involves giving yourself permission to see, rather than expecting that you must know everything. It implies an assumption that if your goal is to be met, you must be the one to see to it, although you will almost always do that in conjunction with others. It means not that you will be perfect, but that you will make an exploration and then shift what does not work. Responsibility means understanding the relationship between what you do and the ultimate results.

People who want to be effective change agents need to take responsibility for everything, even when people at the top do not.

This does not mean to accept blame, to expect yourself to make everything work, or to do everything yourself. It does mean to start out wanting to know what your role in things is. It means to be fascinated by that and take responsibility for it, rather than fearing the worst and looking to cast blame.

Bob's secretary, Marjorie, was very attractive. He thought so, his clients thought so, and she did, too. This was important to Bob. He felt that it conferred a certain status on him. But as Marjorie got more interested in a rewarding career, this quality began to seem less important to her. In fact, she was beginning to think it was hindering her progress.

In Bob's mind a pretty secretary did her job well, flirted, made the coffee and no matter what happened she assured him that everything was all right. Because his focus was not on her, he did not pay much attention to her changing attitude, so when Marjorie asked for a raise, he turned her down without giving it much thought. When she asked for an increase in responsibility, he explained to her that she did not have the background. She was furious and he did not know why. "He thinks of me as a pretty little thing," she said, "He acts nice, but he's no better than the rest. He says, 'Here's a cute little girl. Let's keep her that way.'"

As her department worked with me, she became fascinated by the concept of responsibility. She began to feel that if this situation were going to change, she would have to look honestly at what was happening to her and then take responsibility to change it. She acknowledged that when she got frustrated by a lack of response, she always cooed at her bosses, flirted with them, and sometimes

cried. "When I make a suggestion like a mature professional, I am ignored. When I act all cute and girlish, they
pay attention." But not the attention she had come to want.
At last it was clear to her that waiting for Bob to change
was absurd.

Taking an inventory of the situation, she realized
that she was beginning to call in sick a lot, to do her work
indifferently, and to get into unnecessary power struggles
with coworkers. She decided that an attempt to change
her work environment was necessary. She asked for a facilitated meeting with Bob, explained her reasons for being
upset, and took responsibility for her part in it. She told
him that she did not want to play Barbie Doll anymore and
asked to be trained to take on some more interesting
projects.

They negotiated. Bob agreed to stop the salacious behavior, and he kept his agreement. But he was hard-pressed
to come up with more money for training, and his attempts
to beef up her job ran afoul of another department head
and one of Marjorie's colleagues. Marjorie had not been an
impressive work partner lately. And Bob's heart was not
in it. He had hired a Barbie Doll and that is what he
wanted.

After four months of failed attempts, Marjorie announced that she was taking a job with another company,
one where she would be trained to do the work she wanted
to do. She was going to move to an environment that might
be more conducive to new behavior on her part.

If she is able to remain honest and aware of her tendency to seek
out Barbie Doll roles, Marjorie has a possibility of significant
growth. She understands that she did not create this situation,

nor is she to blame for it; she cannot cure ignorance, or someone's need to make himself feel more important at her expense. But she can change her response to these realities.

## Measuring the Realities

Taking responsibility means making your expectations clear. It also means being willing to measure what is really happening. Most organizations are not adept at measuring their results or their realities. There are too many secrets, the isolation is too great, the fear-driven excuses too numerous.

Barbara was brought into a major food-service corporation from Stanford University just after she had completed her MBA. Her job was to start a quality-assurance program in this old and respected company whose leaders had been embarrassed by some bad press.

"We need new work standards," said the president. So Barbara decided to measure the quality of work being done and determine what needed to be improved. "Not necessary," said the president. "They are doing fine at meeting the old standards. We just need new ones."

But Barbara persisted. She measured performance and discovered that it was at about 65 percent. The president was amazed. Using that information as a foundation, Barbara began an education campaign. She would learn why the standards were not being met and employees would learn more about the standards and why they were important.

At the end of a year she surveyed 250 employees from twenty of the company's outlets across the country. Her goal was to find out if the message of quality was getting down to the line employees. The results were surprising. According to her measures, the great majority of the employees understood the standards very well. It was the company's top brass that did not get the big picture. Employees said management did not give them the resources to meet the standards. They complained of unclear and contradictory instructions, inadequate training, insufficient supplies, and not enough staff. Barbara checked into the charges and came to believe that most of them were accurate. She prepared a report for the next board meeting that listed the problems and proposed some solutions.

"Barbara, Barbara, Barbara," said the chairman, looking up from her report. "We've known about these complaints for twenty years. Employees have always said these things. They always will. That's the way they are." He had no interest in discussing the problems or in responding to them. Following an embarrassed silence, he told her to keep up the good work and then changed the subject. Barbara left the meeting in a white rage, and looking back two years later, she identified that as the moment when she began to think about quitting.

But she stuck with it for a while. Working with employees and managers in the field, she devised standards that might work more effectively and did what she could to improve their resources (furtively at times). She stayed in constant contact with the outlets, modifying standards that did not work, retraining, working with those who felt regulations were applied too rigidly, and acknowledging those whose improvement was impressive. At the end of two years, the standards were being met 83 percent of the time.

But she never got the corporate ear, never got a workable budget, never got the resources the people in the field needed. She came to believe that the guys at the top did not want to know the truth, did not want to measure their results, did not want to respond to problems. "It's responsibility they're afraid of," she remarked. "I can't change that."

## The Responsibilities of Leaders

Responsibility, then, is a vital aspect of the change paradigm. It encompasses being honestly aware of ourselves in the world and it is at the core of what causes human beings to respond wisely to a world that is in constant flux. An organization whose employees feel responsible for the results of their work is one where service is likely to be outstanding. One whose managers are responsible is one whose operations are efficient and creative. And one whose leaders are responsible is likely to produce a product for which there is a genuine need, and to supply its employees with the tools to meet the standards in which it says it believes.

Responsibility among leaders is rare. Acts of honest awareness are not necessarily the qualities that brought about the successful founding of a business. It was more likely the result of being in the right place at the right time, and moving quickly toward a focused goal. And over time, those who run the business succeed because they can maintain things as they are. They conserve. From their perspective it is tempting for them to assume that if they are powerful and wealthy enough, the usual measures of competence and efficiency do not apply to them, that talking about responsibility and mentioning the bottom line often will do the trick.

I know of one company, for example, whose founder built twelve department stores on choice Texas property at a time when land was not expensive. He and then his son ran a tight ship. So tight, in fact, that there were never enough resources to operate the stores properly. One by one the stores failed, and each time they decided to sell off a store, a significant profit was realized because land values had increased. As the company grew less adept at running stores, its wealth increased because its advisors invested the money from the sales wisely. How are the successors to this fortune to understand the relationship between actions and results? How are they to learn that when times change, they and their organization must change?

This inability to see is often compounded by the complexity of the solution. We all sometimes ignore what we assume we cannot handle. It just matters a lot more when leaders do this.

History tells us that this is common. Individuals, organizations, and nations are willing to suffer greatly and die rather than look and respond. Perhaps this is nature's way of replacing old institutions with new ones. In *A Distant Mirror*, historian Barbara Tuchman tells how the French in the late Middle Ages destroyed themselves through a blinding adherence to their chivalrous and ritual way of going to war. In a decisive battle, the English used the Welsh longbow systematically to pick off the flower of French nobility. It was a devastating loss, yet it failed to alert the French that a new day had dawned. The French knew all about the longbow, but they disdained its use as unchivalrous and despised the commoners who used it. After the battle, they did not look at what went wrong and make adjustments. Instead they looked for ways to make chivalry work better. They raised a larger army, increased the weight of the knights' armor (which only made them more vulnerable to a good longbowman), and went out for revenge. Ten years later, their supply of sons renewed, they battled the English again. On the decisive day, the English lost five hundred soldiers and the French lost ten thousand. The French, with their eyes fixed firmly on the past, were still unable to understand what had happened.

## What's the Use?

If the people at the top are unlikely to change, it is difficult for successful change to occur below. This is conventional wisdom. So why should change agents bang their heads against the wall? The answer is clear. You can make a big difference along the way.

> When Barbara announced her decision to leave the food-service corporation, gratifying calls came in from company outlets all across the country. They told her they would miss the attention she gave them. They would miss having a champion. They would miss her way of focusing on something other than short-term goals, and they would miss her way of giving them the benefit of a doubt. Through her engagement with them and her measurement of what was real for them, she had made a big difference. They told her that they had grown as people and that their work had improved.
>
> But she feels that she has failed. "I haven't achieved what I could have," she says. "I know change is a slow process. I know it's painful. But I can't wait until these guys are ready to change. I don't understand why so many people put up with this for years on end. I think the corporate ranks in America are filled with people who don't want to be happy," and she cleaned out her office on her way to going into business for herself.

If you are going to succeed as a change agent, you need to know how bad it is. You need to understand what the limits are and not beat yourself up about it. But you also need to know how to create power and generate growth, how to persevere and how to enjoy it. Acting with integrity—communicating honestly and taking responsibility for what you do—makes a very big difference in this process.

As you and your work group pursue knowledge of how you respond to this challenge, look for first causes of events, seek to recognize what the basic dynamics are, and refuse to wallow in false concerns or side issues. Look for genuine problems to solve, problems whose solutions will take you a step closer to a compelling vision, will provide a great testing ground for your way of handling honesty and responsibility. This approach will establish the foundation for a greater integrity in your relations with colleagues who must join with you if genuine realignments are going to occur between the organization and its environment.

# 6

## Participate Fully in Your Life

It takes a lot of energy to regenerate an organization. It takes a great deal of time, effort, and attention to detail to create a good change strategy and implement it. The people involved must become alert, active, and willing to try something new. Old habits must be broken and comfortable relationships must be shifted. A whole new way of seeing and responding must emerge and a commitment to this new road must be established. Those who are determined to be effective change agents will model this behavior; they will participate actively in the events of their own lives.

This is risky business. The risks include disapproval, confusion, and moving into new territory where the rules are not clear yet, a territory where failure is a distinct possibility. No wonder genuine organization regeneration is so seldom undertaken.

But it is the only path to success. Strategies that are made in the status quo do not produce effective results, while those that emerge from action, that are generated by people who are pushing the boundaries ahead, are more pragmatic and appropriate. These strategies are based on information gathered in the territory where the decisive action will occur and it is new information. They are responsive to evolving forces in the marketplace and they make sense to the people who must implement them.

But strategies that emerge through action can only be created by people who have a particular mind set. People of this sort are open to whatever comes next. The intention that animates them is to see what is real and to respond appropriately, rather than to defend a favorite perspective. Their strategies are lively and growing. They move with events and change when circumstances shift or are revealed more fully over time. Effective change agents participate fully and enthusiastically in their own lives and it is this characteristic that leads to their success.

An organization that successfully implements a comprehensive change strategy is made up of people who think inventively. But this kind of widespread alertness is rare and the result is that most plans, goals, and strategies remain nothing more than good intentions. The follow through never comes and the benefits are never harvested.

The basic lesson to be learned from failed change efforts is that it is impossible to do this work halfheartedly. People at the top cannot expect everyone else to change while they stay stuck in the past. Grafting a lively and flexible group of people onto a moribund organization does not produce long-term gain. Employees cannot be forced to become motivated, nor can an organization be manipulated into a new beginning. Genuine change occurs only when people at every level of the organization finally accept the fact that they must take action themselves.

Those who are able to do this have overcome a number of formidable, age-old obstacles. These barriers live inside each of us, and they are directly tied to our deepest fears, hopes, and yearnings. These forces are so strong that promises, threats, crises, and slogans seldom break through them.

The people who undertake this work must squarely confront the deeper obstacles in themselves, and few of us are willing to do that. It is not surprising then that the greatest attribute shared by successful change agents is that they participate more fully in their own lives than most of us do. This, rather than the push to be the best, an unrelenting desire to make other people change, or the determination to create a particular vision, seems to be the driving force in these masters of change.

## The Nature of Full Participation

Full participation is a difficult but rewarding practice that you must cultivate if you want to make a difference in the organizations you care about. It means being fully engaged in living, responding openly to what life unexpectedly brings to you each day, and shifting your way of doing things when that will elicit more fruitful results.

It does not mean behaving like a cheerleader who has just noticed the television camera, becoming a frantic joiner, always trying to be heard, noticed, or at the head of the charge. There is nothing busy or breathless about this practice. In fact, it often appears in activities such as stopping for a rest or in following someone else's lead. It may mean taking the time to mourn a loss and to recuperate, and it certainly involves pausing often to listen to yourself and others. Above all, it means to come out of isolation where fear, confusion, and shame lie, and to be compelled by relationships to other people and events and by new possibilities. This is no mean feat; it is a rare and wonderful occurrence.

At work it means being able to see beyond the dulling effects of bureaucracy and tradition and to take direct action. It implies being engaged with others in projects that need to be done and discovering ways to avoid unnecessary conflicts. It means finding a balance between being open to spontaneous possibilities on the one hand, and respecting the habitual practices that bring some stability to life and work on the other.

If we were living in a time when obedience rather than innovation was the most important determinant of success, the need for direct engagement with life would not be so urgent for organizations. But our primary institutions are wheezing and misfiring. Leaders find it difficult to compel belief, and we are at a loss for ways to solve our most pressing problems. Even when it seems that we are becoming aware of the depth of the problems, the solutions—even the will to solve them—seem not to be at hand.

This is by no means a hopeless situation, however. If we turn our attention to the way cultures of the past overcame inertia in order to engage in action, history has welcome news for us. Although these problems appear in every historical era, there are times, many of them, when organizations and whole cultures have sprung unexpectedly to life to solve them. Every one of these breakthroughs seemed totally improbable before it happened, the advances it made were surprising and exhilarating, the obstacles it overcame formidable. Looking at how this occurred helps us isolate the practices we can cultivate in order to succeed with this work now. Two stories demonstrate how these problems were perceived by cultures that created magnificent regeneration. Their methods are not antiquated or lost to us. We can do what they did.

## The Dilemma of Overwhelming Odds

Life in Athens at the time of the Battle of Marathon in 490 B.C. is often presented as the height of human courage. It is seen as one of the rare times when hope and confidence rose to the surface so that a people was able to build a profoundly creative society. Classical Greece, which many consider one of the glories of the human story, came to maturity then.

At the time this story takes place, Darius, the Great King of ancient Persia, rules most of the world. His wealth and magnificence are fabulous, his cruelty legendary. The millions under his sway have no say in the way their life is ordered, in how their cities are ruled, or in the distribution of the goods and services they create. Disregard for human suffering marks his rule, and most people accept this as an inalterable fact. They see it as simply the way things are, just as most of us accept the circumstances of our own lives as inevitable.

Nevertheless, revolt breaks out in some cities on the coast of Asia Minor that are subject to the Great King. They cannot hope to counter his might or ferocity, yet in these cities lives an awareness that life can be better, and at length some people take action on this knowledge.

Athens, which is just rising to prominence, sends help to the rebels. When Darius hears of it, he is furious and turns his overwhelming might against Athens. Before long the Great King's army, vast land and sea forces and a huge city of followers, marches to Greece. Ahead of the army are heralds demanding earth and water, the tokens of submission, from the cities on their route. The soldiers drink the rivers dry and devour all the food along the way; they burn cities and change the topography as they advance. Athens is a small obstacle to this giant force.

When Darius's multitudes arrive, the soldiers of Athens stand and give battle. They advance at a run, while the Persians are driven into battle by officers who whip and threaten them, frightening them more than the enemy does. And against all rational calculation, beyond all hope, the Athenian army wins. The Great King's allegedly invincible power is unable to withstand the spirit and the unexpected battle strategy of those who have overcome their own fear and resistance, who know what matters to them, and who are fighting for a way of life they love.

News of this incredible victory flies through the region, and, for the Athenians, life begins to be lived at a more energetic level than it has been. Their sculpture and architecture flower, theater and philosophy develop a new intensity, commerce and private life take on greater creativity. The magnificent Greek way of life is given tremendous impetus that day.

There is a trap in this story, however. It has been used for thousands of years to bludgeon people with the expectation that we should all "give 110 percent," and then move up to *real* effort. It is often used as an example of how we, as opposed to that small Greek army, do not take on the formidable forces, how we are unwilling to give our all.

This is that old song of self-judgment that runs through the back of our minds and is so destructive to living fully. While giving all you have got can be exhilarating and lead to great results, it can also lead to doing more of what has not worked in the past, only doing it harder. It is an idea that often contributes to dogmatic rigidity rather than creative engagement.

But there is another way of looking at the story of Marathon. The Athenian army did what most of us do. They put off honestly looking at the bad news as long as they could, until their peril was so present they were unable to ignore it. Their eventual choice to fight was not extraordinary since not to fight meant death for them, the extinguishing of their way of life.

The first part of the moral then is that you do not have to be a certifiable hero to stand up to overwhelming odds. Ordinary people do it all the time. The anguish the Greeks came to know as the Persian army approached sharpened their spirits and deepened their insights. An amazing victory achieved at the moment when their defeat seemed certain evoked a joyous courage. But they did not lead with this quality; they uncovered it unexpectedly as they acknowledged their fear and moved into action.

As a result of this forced recognition of their own strength, the Greeks were able to see life without the filter of their deepest fears and self-doubt. In them and in their culture was nurtured the wonder of human life, its uncertainty, its possibilities, its beauty and terror and pain. They affirmed the power of humankind to experience reality directly, to hear and do, to speak and create, to acknowledge even the unacceptable in life and to respond. This is the second moral of the story, and it is the glory of human life.

The story captures the way an event, an unexpected discovery, can contribute to a transformation. Another ancient story speaks to the immeasurably more difficult task of facing the daily, mundane forces that stand between us and full engagement with our lives. It is to that story that we turn now.

## Beyond Heroics

The earliest story ever uncovered by anthropologists is the five-thousand-year-old epic of Gilgamesh. It appeared at a transformative moment in human history at a place where the fundamental arts of high civilization were invented. During the early years of this epic, writing, mathematics, monumental architecture, systematic scientific observation, temple worship, and formal government were given to the world. The understanding these people had of how to create value merits attention.

In this story, Gilgamesh is the king of a great city in the ancient Middle East that flourished before the rise of Babylon. He is part man and part god, and his magnificence sets him apart from all others. As a consequence he is thoughtless and unaware of boundaries. He does just what he wants to do no matter who might be hurt. He has no close friends and is not aware that he or anyone else might ever come to die. His potential greatness finds no form or outlet. At length his failure to lead and his practices of bedding down any woman he wants to and of taking the sons of the city off to war on a whim become a terrible burden to those who live in his city, and they pray to the goddess for intercession. The help she sends is marvelous and it transforms human life. She sends him a friend.

She creates a man named Enkidu, who becomes Gilgamesh's great companion. Only Enkidu is a match for Gilgamesh when it comes to strength of body or courage, and through him Gilgamesh learns for the first time to identify with someone else. He learns to love another human being. This love of an equal, this friendship, is the first great gift of the goddess.

The awakened Gilgamesh goes off with his friend on a series of adventures, overcoming obstacles, slaying monsters, and bringing back resources to the people of the city. He has learned to discipline his energies and instead of living unconsciously, he joyously engages in activities that are useful and that benefit others. That is the second gift.

The third gift does not seem like a gift at all. It comes as a result of tragedy. In the course of their adventures, the two heroes anger some of the gods who had liked things as they were. Some of them were fond of the monsters that had been killed; we tend to admire what we create. The heroes' acts infuriate one goddess in particular, who decrees that Enkidu must die. When his friend falls sick and eventually dies, Gilgamesh becomes fully, deeply human for the first time. Unable to understand what is happening, he is consumed by grief and sorrow, he is out of his mind with suffering.

Gilgamesh's grief is the third and greatest gift of the goddess. With grief comes compassion, an emergence from isolation and self-absorption. This first real awareness of what it is to be human leads him to seek the plant of eternal life. He sets out to find it and bring it back to his city so that others will no longer suffer as he has.

Again he endures many ordeals and overcomes great obstacles, but at length he locates the plant, and immediately after plucking it from the ocean's floor and swimming to shore, he falls into an exhausted sleep. When he awakens, he sees a serpent slithering away from him, a serpent that has just devoured the plant. This serpent sloughs its skin (the first of many sloughings) and goes on to live an eternal life.

Gilgamesh returns home, disconsolate, and, he thinks, defeated. But on his way he remembers the words of Siduri the wine maiden, whom he had encountered earlier. It was she, he now knows, who spoke the truth, and her words become the great gift he takes back to his people.

> Gilgamesh, where are you hurrying to? You will never find that life for which you are looking. When the gods created man they allotted to him death, but life they retained in their own keeping. As for you, Gilgamesh, fill your belly with good things; day and night, night and day, dance and be merry, feast and rejoice. Let your clothes be fresh, bathe yourself in water, cherish the little child that holds your hand, and make your wife happy in your embrace; for this too is the lot of man.

Gilgamesh was delivered from meaninglessness through the gifts of friendship, contribution, grief, and, above all, the simple pleasures of a fully lived daily life. They deliver us just as they did the people of the ancient Middle East who loved this story for thousands of years. The capacity of these gifts to transform personal lives and the life of organizations has not changed in more than five millennia.

## The Dynamics of Procrastination

The stories of the Battle of Marathon and Gilgamesh are a priceless inheritance from our ancestors. They suggest ways we can create institutions that keep us in touch with our deeper selves, with one another, and with a changing world. They tell us how to regenerate relationships, organizations, and cultures. The story of Marathon tells us what was done, while the Epic of Gilgamesh shows how it was accomplished.

In both of these examples of creative regeneration, the people involved grudgingly faced up to reality. They stopped the excuses and the halfhearted attempts, and they took a good look at the awful truth. This is where we must start as well.

But what was the crucial factor in this transformation? Just what was it they finally came to grips with? It is something deeper than the particular problems or circumstances they were concerned with at the time crisis came to their lives. In both stories it is the awareness of death. At the heart of the emotions that keep us isolated and ignorant of our own existence is the universal human awareness that someday we will die, and that this event is not negotiable, nor something we can predict or alter.

This knowledge can overwhelm. It can numb us to what is happening because of the sense that the outcome of human life is preordained and no amount of hard or good work will alter that fact. This awareness is not debilitating as long as a system of belief is intact that tells us that there is some greater meaning to our activities, that those who govern us or direct our work do it well and wisely and that the system that chooses and guides these leaders does so in our interest, with the result that our life is better for it. But when those conditions are absent, when we do not trust our institutions or leaders, when belief is uncertain, then we are easily susceptible to a deep and enervating malaise.

This might seem a little extreme, so let me be clear. I do *not* mean that if at the office Larry is late with his report, you should inquire softly if he was so distracted by the fear of death that he was unable to work adequately. Or that you should take the afternoon off to comfort him if he says yes, in fact, that is the very reason. I mean that it is time to stop pretending that we can deal with deep and complex problems in a superficial fashion. Genuine engagement with the real, changing world is an effective antidote to any fear, but it will only occur when we bring the deepest forces that animate our lives to the experience.

As long as the deeper issues are not engaged, our efforts will be timid and inadequate, and we will spend most of our time procrastinating and looking for someone else to blame. Learning how to live fully and openly, on the other hand, is the key to reaping the rewards that accompany coming to grips with reality.

What the awareness of mortality means to us in our attempt to do this is interesting. Steven Levine, in his book *Who Dies: An Investigation of Conscious Living and Dying*, puts it succinctly when he says, "If we examine our fear of death we see in it a fear of the moment to follow, over which we have no control. In it is a fear of impermanence itself, of the next unknown changing moment of life."

It means that when we become unconsciously obsessed with postponing death, we postpone whatever is next. We postpone life. Anytime we are faced with significant uncertainty or failure, with disapproval, being wrong, or not being chosen, we experience it as extinction of the person we want to be. That is terrifying because we count on this ideal person to control events. We come to feel that if only we are perfect or good, if we win or prevail, if we are accepted or loved completely we will not suffer and die. Or that we will succeed in putting those experiences off into the distant future.

Because we have a limited ability to control the outcomes that matter most to us, we develop elaborate fantasies about how we should be and about how life should be. The flaws we see in ourselves seem to be fatal. Many of our thoughts and feelings are turned into a secret shame, and we blame ourselves when things do not go right. We hide from bad news. We hide from *good* news. We hide from whatever might be next in our lives. We go to war with ourselves.

As a result of this internal struggle, we spend a lot of time mourning the loss of what might have been. We mourn for the person we are but refuse to acknowledge, and for the life we are in but are not experiencing.

But whatever we deny or resist begins to dominate our activities. We surround ourselves with a wall of fears and judgments, and we focus on it obsessively, constantly vigilant, guarding that wall as if our lives depended on it. All this resistance causes great pain; it dulls us and debilitates us. This is as true of organizations as it is of the people within them. When Gilgamesh and the Marathon warriors faced this condition squarely, they touched a great internal strength. As a result, they found themselves in action in a way that brought great value to their cultures. The action they took, their mythological journey, is available to us as well.

In the modern world, we tend not to have well-developed myths to guide us in this way; nor do we have heroes whose lives of overcoming difficulties allegorically parallel our own. Our stories state the problem and then they sort of peter out without resolution. But even these stories help us develop ways to move into action because they provide us with a sense of recognition. They tell us how things are for us and what obstacles need to be handled. That recognition is the prelude to effective action.

So before discussing how historical knowledge can help us overcome the modern version of this old dilemma, we will look at a contemporary myth that conveys a common message today that tells us where we are. When you read it, remember that the power of any myth lies in seeing it as your own story. You can use it to explore your own philosopher's road map.

## The Curse of the Bambino

The Boston Red Sox have not won a World Series since 1918. Red Sox fans are long suffering, in fact suffering is a central tenet in this team's mystique. Although this is true with every sports team, Red Sox fans are masters of this emotion.

The story goes that the year after winning that last glorious series, they traded the great Babe Ruth—the Bambino—to the New York Yankees and ever since that monumentally stupid move they have been cursed. This curse dictates that it is impossible for them ever to win another World Series.

In the years when the Red Sox field strong teams, discussions of the curse begin to emanate from Boston by mid-season. The expectation is that the Sox will eventually suffer humiliating defeat just when everyone's hopes have been fanned to their highest pitch. So strong is this belief, so religiously is it repeated, that it lodges eventually in the hearts of players, and events always turn out as predicted. Every victory increases the fear of defeat, robbing players of their concentration, tiring them with worry, turning joy into foreboding. It distorts perceptions so that small problems along the way seem like huge obstacles.

This fear isolates players from their natural emotions and from their teammates. Life seems unfair, as if fate were staying up nights thinking of ways to torment the Red Sox and their fans. Opponents play against them with unusual confidence because they know what will happen. Calls go against them because officials see what they expect to see. And when they fall behind, the Red Sox become subdued and preoccupied.

This long-running melodrama always has the same unhappy ending. A particular kind of defeat is sustained, one that gets to be perversely rewarding to the faithful. They know it will happen and it hurts, but at least they are not alone in their sorrow. They are united with all the good-hearted, long-suffering Red Sox fans who have shared this curse for more than seventy-five years.

History is full of great curses that afflict whole peoples, and the effect is always to reinforce a devastating paralysis. While this sort of belief holds sway, people are severely limited in their capacity to take effective action or to respond spontaneously to the events of their lives. Each time our ancestors rose from their torpor, on the other hand, they did it by facing up to what was at the root of their problems and opportunities. Only then were they able to challenge the limiting beliefs that prevailed in the culture, beliefs that inhibited spontaneity, growth, and coordinated action. Only then was the power tapped that allowed them to tackle the particular curse of the times.

## Our Little Soldiers

In our world there is no overarching belief to direct our attention away from ourselves and back to the big picture. So we experience this curse daily in the form of obsessions about failure, not being right, not being appreciated. We fall easy prey to fights, misunderstandings, and power struggles, and happily put aside activities that would lead to effective action. Any time people get to thinking in these starkly individual terms, problems seem enormous and overwhelming.

Why would anyone want to live a life that is so precarious, where every day the chances of being totally blotted out are very high? Nobody wants that kind of life. Instead we create a personal epic myth with its own private hero. These heroes are isolated and weak, but they are seldom surprised and they persist no matter what happens. Our personal heroes are not extinguished by fear, failure, embarrassment, or rejection, because these depredations are what they expected all along. Each defeat only shows how right they are about life. And unlike the traditional heroes who were public figures, these heroes do not bring life-affirming gifts back to their communities. They are loners, and like the Red Sox, they are doomed perpetually to fail.

Most of us created these little soldiers when we were children. Everyone in our families had a little soldier, and they always did the same thing no matter what new experiences life dished up. Pretty soon our own soldiers did, too.

Is it surprising then that by the time we are old enough to go to work, we have gotten to be experts at playing this character and that we trot it out constantly? It is so effective and fast acting at obliterating uncertainty and pain that we reach for it as we would a powerful pain-relieving medication. It gets to be an addiction, a mind-altering internal drug that makes reality go away. But living inside these soldiers is frustrating. They can never have an authentic and spontaneous relationship, certainly not with other little soldiers. We often feel trapped inside this character, because we are never flexible in there.

Hoping that a bunch of little soldiers working in an organization will look realistically at circumstances and act appropriately is futile. At times of uncertainty and anxiety, you can walk into an office and it is fantasy land. It is total animation. The room is full of these characters performing their roles intensely, and as long as this is true, neither personal nor organizational goals are being sought with any degree of effectiveness.

## Inside the Fortress

Our soldiers live in heavily guarded fortresses. Inside these walls, a council of generals determines how life is interpreted. They first did this years ago and they see no reason to change now. They perpetuate the status quo by severely limiting the information allowed in. This guard work is exhausting and the costs are high, which means that huge defense budgets are required. The result is that this defensive structure is so limited in its capacity to receive and process information that it is almost always at odds with external reality. It cannot tell us much about events and people, or about our own needs.

Living in this fortress limits our ability to grow naturally and compromises our principles. Our participation in this restricted life supports the painful state of conflict in which we are embroiled, which in turn strengthens the power of the fortress. It is not harmless activity. Each time we listen to this internal voice that defines how things are or how they should be, we limit our ability to experience events as they really are. We all spend years doing this and paying the price. Eventually, however, the conflicts that this false image engenders may become so painful that we want to be free.

## Leaving the Fortress

The first step in breaking out of the fortress is acknowledging how bad it is and that another way of doing things is available to us. This is an easy process to start, and once we do, our soldiers always get wind of our discontent. After trying every form of fear and intimidation in their considerable arsenals, the sly dogs offer to help. They make suggestions and propose courses of action. Consequently these first steps of recognition are shaky and confusing. Sometimes we hear the voice of a part of ourselves that wants to emerge and see what is going on out there, and sometimes it is a soldier that wants to terrify us back into the fortress. Deciding which one to listen to is never easy. When we finally decide that the pain and fear, the conflicts and self-denial have become too big a price to pay for being right about the world's unfairness, we know what to expect. We will be badly shaken, our soldiers will protest and fight. We will feel vulnerable and be hurt in our own special ways.

But this remains a vital and rewarding process. It is a wonderful opportunity to get acquainted with the parts of ourselves we have been hiding, and to learn more about the mechanisms we use to keep ourselves from fully engaging with life. Here is an exercise to move you along in this work. It begins with that old ploy of procrastinators, making a list. In this case, note three examples from each of the following:

- the people who annoy you most right now
- the things that make you angriest
- the things you fear most
- the events that have seemed most unfair in your life
- the way you feel when you fail at something
- the ways you usually have your feelings hurt
- your favorite ways of getting sympathy

These items are crucial aspects of your epic story—reflections of the rigid life view generated inside your fortress—and they represent a partial measure of the distance between you and the living truth. These are images you will cling to in order to deflect life; they are the strength of your soldier and the building blocks of your fortress. You will focus on them in order not to look beyond, to hide from knowing what your life can be.

The point is not to know these upsetting images in order to hate them, or even to change them. It is actually something quite different. It is to take a good look at what is there—to know that this is part of you and to accept it. This means, for example, that each instance of fear or anger can be explored in its fullness rather than being the trigger for shame or revulsion. Through this process we may eventually come to feel at home with ourselves as we are less and less at war. It is not the truth that hurts. It is the rigid denial of it and the assumption that it is shameful and wrong.

When these distressing feelings make their way to the surface, you may go into isolation, run back into the fortress, hide behind your soldier. Everyone does this. But it is useful to know about these reactions and not to be driven unconsciously by them. First begin to notice the prices paid for each one: the arguments, the misunderstandings, the hurt feelings, the fatigue, and the limitations on fun, enjoyment, and success. Then it is possible to know the things you can do differently to get results that are more gratifying.

These feelings and behaviors are only part of your truth and knowing them intimately presents you with a choice. The choice is to react to the triggering event with the habitual response or with one of the others you have at hand. It can be very pleasant not to carry this one-response burden around all the time, and not to be stopped from dealing with the task at hand because of triggering events that are superfluous.

If I am making this sound easy, do not be deceived. This is the stuff of heroes; it is what the Greek soldiers overcame at Marathon and it is Gilgamesh's struggle. But eventually, with discipline and courage, you will overcome this prepossessing set of responses just as they overcame their limited vision of life. And, just as they did, you will acknowledge as real what had previously not been acceptable.

Yet, if it is the stuff of heroes, it is something that everyone has done, and this will become clearer with each act of embracing reality. We have all overcome a great list of obstacles. Acknowledging this is also a part of knowing what is real. Take a few moments now to list some of the obstacles you have overcome. They may have to do with disease or misfortune; they may be work related or personal. They may be big and dramatic or they may appear to be relatively minor. But they all matter.

## Reaching Out

Participating fully means to keep breaking through the barriers. Over and over again. Learn to ask for support from someone capable of giving it. Learn to say here is how I feel. Here is what triggers me. Here is what I request from you. Here is what I take responsibility for.

While it is crucial to know that there are other ways of doing things, however, and that they can be rewarding, expecting ourselves to do all this alone is self-defeating. It is impossible. The transforming moment in every historical account comes when people emerge from isolation and fear and reach out to one another.

Dialogue heals. Honest, supportive groups build new personal expectations and partnerships that do not thrive on anticipatory breakdown. In these groups you do not spend time justifying yourself, being right, or making others wrong. Moreover, when your soldier reappears and *it* happens again, nobody is surprised or disappointed. They expect it, accept it, and move on to what is next.

In this part of the journey we are still uncertain that we want to break out of the fortress. And, of course no human being ever entirely breaks away from his or her past, overcomes every bad habit or unfortunate appetite. The old home in the fortress will always be there and even the most enlightened among us revisit it from time to time. It is not surprising, then, that during the first stages of the struggle to break free, we may want to face up to the awful truth, but we still want it to be someone's fault.

## Taking Risks

When you break out of the fortress, you take risks. You risk the loss of the security that seemed to be present inside, by trying new behavior that might not work. You are vulnerable and open to other people. No wonder we put the breakout off as long as we can.

Ellen was always cool. Her defenses were never down. Her pose was world weary and cynical. She was not going to get overly excited about any job—certainly not the one she

presently held. She went out of her way to demonstrate
her detachment, her superiority to it. She did not bother to
get the details right, was rude to coworkers, and made it a
point to dress sloppily. She had been warned and disciplined
repeatedly and it only made her more cynical, more right
about how the world was determined not to respect her.

On the day before her vacation, the boss took her aside.
"There are two Ellens who come to work here," she said.
"One of them is rude and sloppy; the other is creative and
dresses with dignity. The rude, sloppy one is not welcome
back. If she returns, she will go on probation. I'd be delighted to welcome the other one back."

Tough stuff. A wake-up call with choices clear as a bell.
It got Ellen's attention and she thought long and hard about
it during her vacation. She later reported going through a
lot of turmoil, some anger and resentment, a fear of losing a
job she needed very badly, and much more.

But she was ready for a change. This tough-guy posture
was exhausting. She had been at it for years and every time
she assumed it she took a beating. Her friends and family
had talked to her about it. Now she had the opportunity to
try out new behavior. Her department was working on
building cohesion and confidence. They had agreed to find
systems to make work more efficient and pleasant. Other
people were acknowledging that they could change, so she
decided to test the waters of change, too.

She returned from her vacation when a staff meeting
was scheduled and burst into the room looking great. She
said, "Lisa said that there are two Ellens who work here
and I didn't realize that. She asked me to choose which one
would come back. I think you can all see which one is here.
I love looking good, actually, and I'll keep looking like this."

When she took the significant risk of dropping her
cynical posture, she found that it had been a package deal.

When her appearance improved, her rudeness declined and so did her sloppiness in doing the tasks associated with her work. Because she had taken the risk, and taken it with the support of her work group, she was able to open up to a much richer, fuller experience on the job. She accepted this as her job, and herself as the person doing it. She lightened up, was less rigid, and began to make a contribution.

Ellen could not have done this on her own. She needed the wake-up call and she needed support, both the initial support and the continuing support to keep at it when the temptations to return to her cynical character were overwhelming. This may not sound heroic to you, but it does to me. Ellen took on a great challenge, she handled it courageously and with grace, and she created value for other people in the process.

## Knowing How Bad It Really Is

Every wake-up call is a form of feedback, and opening up to it is a crucial activity at every stage in the journey. Feedback is everywhere and it comes in infinite forms. Distressing in its invariability, it tells us that we have been passing off the same story or two for years with deadly and boring regularity. It is excruciatingly hard to accept this without feeling like a fool. But heroes listen anyway and get over themselves. They reach out to others and discover that most of the terrible secrets they harbored were known to the people around them, and that these people were obsessed by their own terrible secrets.

After a period of walking with this knowledge, a new territory opens up on our philosopher's map. In this land we learn how bad it really is. And it is worse than we originally thought. Here is where we make the discovery that we are really human, deeply, fatally human. Here is where we realize that all the things we have been facing and admitting are really true. We begin to see that it cannot be fixed. It is so bad that there is nothing to hide any more and nothing to protect. It becomes a relief just to accept it.

This information, when it finally comes to us, can be exhilarating. It would previously have hurt our feelings, threatened our sense of safety, but it has curiously little impact now. In fact, seeing how free we can be from compulsive defensiveness in the face of it is a delightful experience. Getting to this place is not fun, of course; it is one of a hero's most difficult trials. But just as the heroes in the myths do, we reach the point where we like the challenge and we begin to seek it regularly.

There are times in the workplace when my colleagues and I feel that people are ready for an extraordinary breakthrough of this sort. This usually happens when the going has been especially rough, when work conditions are far from ideal, when there has been a lot of confusion and people have been at each other's throats. A final condition is that the players are genuinely committed to shifting their own behavior in order to improve the situation.

At a small Midwestern manufacturing company I organized a retreat for the embattled executive committee. I told them to expect the hard stuff. And they came prepared.

After two days of building trust, confidence, and commitment, I asked them to select a partner and to sit across from that person, knees nearly touching. They were asked to choose a partner A who would talk first, while partner B listened like a hawk. Partner A was asked to take three minutes to finish the following sentence: "Sometimes when we work together it doesn't go very well. At those times what concerns me about working with you is . . ."

This exercise was particularly designed for two powerful executives who had been slashing each other up rather
mercilessly. This was an opportunity to get down and really
say it. More than that, it was an opportunity for each of them
to hear how bad it really was from the person who knew it
best. And they did not disappoint. Each, in his turn, said it
all clearly and forcefully. The episode was intense and
earnest but not angry or dramatic.

The next step was for the partners to finish a sentence
that began, "Sometimes when we work together it goes very
well, and at those times what I like about working with you
is . . ." And that too was a revelation for both executives as
they began to note a number of similarities and some
respect.

Finally, they were asked to complete a sentence that
began, "My goal in working with you is . . ." The depth of
each one's answers impressed the other.

The two executives emerged from this session a little
awestruck, as if they had survived a great battle. Each one
knew that he had heard some hard truths, each was reminded that his interlocutor was bright, formidable, and had no
intention of going away, and both knew that they would be
able, if the circumstances were right, to shift the behavior
that was getting them in trouble.

This was a serious, attention-grabbing incident for both
of them, and when a shocking intervention occurred, the
power of the exchange became evident. As the members of
the committee were sitting down for lunch, a message came
for one of the parties to this struggle. He was called to the
phone, where he learned that his father had just died. He
took a long walk on the terrace and prepared to go to his
father's house, but before leaving he sent a message to the

man who had just confronted him. "Tell Al," he said, "that he was incredible this morning. I really respect what he had to say. And tell the rest of the team that I am excited by what we are doing here."

The exercise the two executives had shared is one that brings participants who are honestly willing to play to an unusual state of recognition. It is a process that evokes self-respect and compassion. Taking the risk of hearing what is real about ourselves is to move away from our soldier and its myth, out of the fortress, and on to the border of the unknown. It is here, when we allow ourselves to move with openheartedness and courage, that life reveals its fullness.

In our daily activities we often lose the sense of who we are. We have forgotten that we, too, are the truth. In all our various aspects, we are nature's truth—including the parts we don't like, those we admire, and others we never imagined. This knowledge is where growth lives. It is not a place where happiness replaces fear and sorrow, but it is the home of creativity, gratification, and joy.

## The Road to Compassion

Seeing ourselves as others do is one of the processes of philosophy, one of the mechanisms of self-knowledge. Plato said this practice evokes an eros, a wish to connect. That is why self-exploration has such a powerful capacity to intervene in the denigration and fear that paralyze us. It leads to compassion, the state of mind that surfaced in Parzival so that he was at last able to heal the ailing king, and it moves others to discover and communicate similar processes in themselves.

If we are willing to pause for a few moments to look at our self-judgments as if these were characteristics in someone else whom we respect, we just might be able to feel some compassion for ourselves. We might see our way clear to stop fighting unnecessary battles over the things we use to hurt or frighten ourselves, over image, irritations, and insults. Once this has occurred, we can stop holding our breath, we can stop waiting to be understood or accepted or loved enough. We can relax and start living our lives fully.

## A Hero for Our Times

These activities are part of a long-term process. They are a series of events that accrue and become a rewarding journey. Although Fairway Fred would scoff to hear it, his is such a story. He did it all. He faced up to the truth, reached out, risked new behavior, began to discover compassion for himself and others, and he took action that created unexpected value. Fairway Fred is a hero.

> Fairway Fred is independent and confident. John Wayne could have taken his correspondence course. He is the director of a Florida resort and he is a great success. The place is friendly, efficient, and well run. But it was not always that way, and neither was Fred.
>
> He was overwhelmed when he was first put in charge. He had no experience running a resort or being a boss. More than that, he did not like talking to people, he did not know how to do it, and every meeting was terrifying to him. Learning how to work with his staff was the hardest job he ever had. He was uncomfortable being out front and accountable. He liked to be off on his own, and it was difficult for him to reach out, to keep in contact, especially when things did not go well. His natural tendency at times such as that was to yell a lot and then go off alone.

"When I first came here, I was afraid to tell them that I did not know how to be a boss. I looked around for somebody who could help me figure it out. The natural one was my boss, but he yelled at me so much I thought that was how you were supposed to manage. So I got tough with my guys; I yelled at them a lot. Before long I had a rebellion on my hands, we started to have union problems, and they were not working very hard. I felt like I had failed."

Fred's worst fears had come true. Afraid that if he began to talk to his staff he would look like a fool, he did just that. But Fred was lucky. He was able to find other role models. "I started talking to other directors, and they told me I had to calm down if I didn't want to screw everything up. I spent time asking these guys questions and watching how they did it. I took some management seminars and I changed."

"That made a big difference. I learned how to talk with my staff and I started to enjoy being a manager. I liked solving problems and working with other guys when the pressure was on. This was all new for me."

As his relationship with his staff grew more effective, the quality of their work improved, and Fred was able to move on to other important tasks. He grew less self-conscious and more spontaneous. He began working to get the resources necessary to make the resort a first-rate place.

"The corporate guys told me I was an idiot for wanting to spend money to renovate this place, but after years of making suggestions and giving them documentation, they finally agreed. It takes time and money to turn a place around. It took five years for me to turn this one around, and part of that was because I made a lot of mistakes and I was afraid to admit it. It took another five years for the reputation to catch up. But it finally did, and now we are known as one of the best-managed resorts in the region."

As most of us do, Fairway Fred began his journey without knowing it. Facing the fact that things were not working brought him
to recognition. Seeing that there was another way to go about it
helped him find the strength to open up to new possibilities. As
he went for it again and again, he discovered the healing power of
action and its capacity to attack despair and isolation. As he failed
and tried again, he continually discovered himself—his urges, his
abilities, his contributions.

Although Fred did not know it, he was following one of the
practices essential to creating deep changes, and he tapped resources he never knew he had. As he learned to stay fully
engaged, he began instinctively to accept his inheritance, to walk
the road that his hero ancestors had walked.

When we break out of isolation this way, the gifts we receive
are miraculous. And then, beyond all hope, we discover our
deeper selves, our true individuality, and we are ready to make
our unique contribution.

# 7

## Express Yourself

Creating a successful transition is a little like fortune telling. It seems to require reading the future. Responding wisely to forces that are just beginning to emerge is a complex task requiring subtle abilities. Where do we find these abilities and how do we manifest them?

The answer, of course, is that these abilities already live in us and learning to recognize them is the beginning. Learning to use them effectively is the next step, and working with others who are doing the same is the last. It is not the future we need to read. It is ourselves.

People who contribute significantly to transitions have discovered a part of themselves that knows a great deal about life. This discovery is so gratifying that they are able to stop being upset that they are not perfect or cannot do everything in sight and they are able to enjoy themselves. They find themselves more often in action, and they become more effective.

To reach this point you must learn to express yourself. Acknowledge the parts of yourself that are wise and capable. Only then can you be who you truly are, know your special contribution and make it.

By this time, you know that expressing yourself does not mean always telling people how angry you are or how unfairly you are being treated, although these may be important aspects of getting to know yourself and the world you live in. Nor does it mean that in looking deeply at yourself you will uncover only wisdom and beauty. This deeper knowledge comes only to those who embrace all of themselves, whether it is attractive or not. Nor do these deeper expressions come into the world in the form of great dialogues; you can make them with your mouth shut. It means that you exude qualities that are central to your being. It may mean that you work hard at tasks and love getting the details right. It may mean that you have an unusual capacity for friendship and keeping relationships open and effective. It may mean that you are inventive and creative.

Whatever form it takes, this self-knowledge leads to a bold but deft inventiveness that has marked every era of regeneration in human history. The results can be magnificent, but you do not have to run around, tongue hanging out, being magnificent all the time. When you know yourself, you can begin to accept the fact that you can only make your own contribution, not everyone else's as well. You know that this contribution is enough and that your task is to find it, reveal it, and experience it.

## Discovering the Covenant

If you have followed the practices I recommend, you will have been on a journey of radical experimentation. By the time this fifth practice kicks in, you will be trying many possible selves on for size, auditioning them to determine their attributes and their appeal. Excitement and depression alternate disconcertingly while this is happening. The people around you seem to be either angels or demons. Your experiences seem to be either triumphs or disasters.

This journey is like adolescence. You have left your old home, the place where you learned your values, and every time you try something new, the internalized voices call out from the recesses of the fortress to say that you are wrong. You feel badly about striking out on your own and you are easily confused just as Parzival was. "Only now," said Parzival, "do I realize how long I have been wandering with no sense of direction and unsustained by any happy feelings." It's important to have support around at this juncture so that you do not feel isolated and disoriented. But when the transition is being experienced by the whole organization or culture and the basic assumptions about life are coming into question, it is difficult to find that support.

When the old paradigm is intact, it generates principles that seem adequate. But as life changes more swiftly than the paradigm and the principles begin to falter in their capacity to produce solutions to deep problems, it seems for a while as if there are no guiding concepts. Free experimentation is necessary now if you are going to discover who you are under all your armor and if you are going to look at what actions the new realities require. So you must find another source of wisdom and constancy that will guide you according to some affirmative and ordering principles.

These principles will come from outside the paradigm, from a veneration of life that may best be described as a covenant. A covenant begins with a sense of gratitude, an appreciation of gifts: the gift of life, the wisdom of our ancestors, the cultural legacies that guide us through difficult times. These concepts loom large in the territory you are now entering.

Because the old paradigm is not enough, you may see through the holes in it to something far deeper and more generative. You may glimpse some of the principles that are the classic underpinnings of human life. Knowledge of these principles grows out of the remembrance, as Plato said, of who you really are. This powerful recognition is available to anyone who accepts it.

The principles that breathe life into the covenant are simple and clear. But to know them requires knowing yourself. This knowledge is nurtured by compassion and generosity and it shuns contempt and cynicism. It gains strength as those who discover this gift share it, and it thrives as they work together on projects that create sensible new responses to life's changing requirements. This covenant can be experienced directly as the gifts nature gave you, from your life itself to your personal characteristics to the values you cherish. It releases in you a powerful sense of self-acceptance and belonging. It will be crucial to your confidence and integrity as you travel the roads that ribbon the territory of transition. These unique gifts can be found and articulated in your work group and this will be one of its most valuable functions. But this is not easy work. Most of us resist this good news mightily.

## But What If Who You Are *Is* Unacceptable?

One of the reasons both individuals and organizations do not want to look deeply at who they are is the fear of discovering a monster living in there. I have never seen it happen. The monsters I have encountered in this work are all on the surface. They are products of the struggle to suppress who we are. We have all been told at some point in our lives that our deepest needs and feelings are inappropriate, and we tend to confuse this with being not all right inside. This fifth practice is designed to cut through that territory, but for some people, who they are is not all right with many others, and the problems they encounter on their journey to discover themselves are more complex.

I once heard a woman describe this phenomenon perfectly. When she was a little girl, she looked in the mirror one day and was stricken with horror. Something she had long suspected was obviously true. She was black. It hit her hard. "Oh, no," she exclaimed. "I'm one of them." Although she later came to recognize this information as good news, the moment of acknowledging that she was different from the great mass of people around her was difficult.

To some extent, the search for who we are must always be done in defiance of cultural and organizational life. And if you fall into one of the categories that the culture defines as undesirable, your path can be perilous.

Yet in some way or other, we are all *one of them.* We waste time hiding the fact and fearing to know how different we are. These fears are the great friend of isolation; they are inimical to self-knowledge and are death in a pluralistic society or in an organization that wants to be effective in a diverse world. The negative generalizations and prejudices about being different that we project on others and ourselves are preposterous, and they can only be maintained with great application and hard work. This takes a lot of time, wears a lot of people out, makes a lot of work impossible, and hurts a lot of people.

"They're hiring a fag!" said Bob aghast. "Do you believe it? That's all I need in my department."

Asked why this upset him, he replied in injured tones that this job called for toughness and discipline. How did they think this guy could handle it? He would get no respect and would be wiped out by the first crisis. He would make everyone's life more difficult.

And it turned out that the new employee demonstrated almost all the characteristics Bob had predicted and he did not last a year. The only point he missed on was sexual orientation. The new guy hit on Bob's secretary his first week on the job, which made sense to everybody and the "accusation" was forgotten. Bob never had to notice the distance between his judgments and reality, and he did not learn anything about how to select employees or what it took to do the job well.

Next time Bob sets out to hire someone, he will not know why the last hire failed. He is likely to pick the wrong straight guy and refuse to pick the right gay one. A lot of Bob's actions are irrelevant to getting the job done. They indicate that Bob is afraid to know who he really is and how he is unique. Every assault he participates in takes him more deeply into hiding and he probably does not know it. Watching the anxiety that marks people's relationships with those they see as significantly different from themselves is a valuable course in learning how much we fear knowing the parts of ourselves that we consider hidden and dangerous.

Peggy is a charming, hard-working professional. Unfailingly pleasant but tough, she inherited a department that had a lot of improving to do and she set out to make it great.

Two of the women on her small staff were black and she took them under her wing. She told them how to dress, set out to improve their work habits, and made up a new office code of behavior. She found their work lacking in a certain attention to detail, but told them that she knew it was not their fault since they came from backgrounds where excellence probably was not so important as it had been in hers. They gulped their anger down when she talked like that and tried to ignore it. But she had no conscious awareness that she was being offensive since it was not mentioned, and she sailed along from blunder to blunder.

Then she began to go too far too often. She limited their husbands' access to the office (one of them came to pick up his wife wearing shorts). Then one of the women wore a dress to the office one day that was so diaphanous that from a certain angle in the sunlight the outline of legs could be discerned. "We're selling services in this department Janice," she said, "but not *that* sort of service."

That remark did it. The women asked for a facilitated meeting so they could tell Peggy what they felt was going on and to make it clear that this was unacceptable to them. They were asked exactly what was unacceptable, and for the first time since these episodes had begun a year earlier, the awful *R* word was said in public. Peggy is a racist, they replied.

When the facilitator approached Peggy with the request for a meeting, she was shattered. Not clear on the concept, she nevertheless knew that it was not nice to be called a racist and she was furious. All she could think about was how hard she had tried to improve these womens' professional skills, the trouble she had taken for them, and how much she cared. When the facilitator urged her to look at her role in this situation, and to take responsibility for what she did that was not working as well as for the caring, she refused. She would attend a meeting. But take the rap for being a racist? Over her dead body.

At the meeting, a split second after the facilitator laid out the ground rules, Peggy went on the offensive. What was being said behind her back, she told them, had been made known to her and she could not work with people who made such horrible accusations. She was angry and frightened, but clear and forceful. She demanded an apology.

Under ordinary circumstances her staff would have been abashed, but this was a matter of their deepest values, this was their personal territory. So her secretary, Louise, thanked her for coming to the point directly and acknowledged saying that Peggy was racist. "I want this office to work," added Louise, "and I'm not a vindictive person. I just want you to know that you act that way. I'll comply with your instructions that my husband not come around, and I won't bring my children here either because I won't subject them to that sort of treatment. But I want you to hear me tell you that this is racist."

Peggy began to cry. "But I'm not like that. I'm a nice person," she said. "Yes, you are a nice person," replied Louise, "and I know that you care about us, but you're also a racist."

This was a new one to Peggy! Having it acknowledged that she was a nice person took some of the pressure off. She could see that the level of emotional violence that would be directed back at her would be bearable and she was able to move a step toward taking responsibility for her part in this.

"Well, what do you mean by racist?" she asked.

"In your case it means that you have a narrow perspective. You have accepted a set of ideas that you haven't explored and you don't look at us as real people. Some of the things you say and do just knock the wind out of me and I spend a lot of time fighting off the anger. I'd rather spend the time getting something done around here."

The ground had shifted and they began to have an interesting conversation. Peggy was amazed at what she was hearing, and she began to see some validity in the picture they painted of her. She wanted to know more. This was vitally important information to her if she did not want to continue being blindsided by her unexplored beliefs. And in the calm atmosphere that emerged, she discovered that these women, in turn, really wanted to learn the professional skills she could teach them. That mattered very much to Peggy.

Some measures were agreed to. They would educate Peggy about what they perceived as racist activities and she would set out goals and standards for the office. A lot of knowledge was exchanged in the next several months and horizons were expanded. Haltingly they began to get along better. Peggy calmed down a great deal, and her two employees began to do work that impressed her.

But the final results were not happy ones. This department was a pressure spot. Peggy's immediate supervisor had an impossible job and he often used Peggy's department as a scapegoat. The constant pressure without the possibility of being heard kept the stress level high in the department. And in the end, they all discovered that when racism declines, people who are largely without power and who are being pitted against one another still do not work together well.

We are all, in some way, subject to this sort of systematic assault, and the pressures of organizational life often encourage us to participate in it—to attack and then hide ourselves. We are abused and we abuse others for reasons that are without foundation. It is an unending chain that undermines self-knowledge, and it can stop a healthy transition dead in its tracks. Peggy and her employees were caught in this web, and so was her boss, who chose to scapegoat the whole department rather than look at his real options.

The antidote to this dilemma is to stay the course, to continue working to know who you are, and to honor your roots, which are nourished by the covenant available to us all.

The restaurant manager was from the old school. Bill was tough but affectionate with his employees. He was an Irishman and most of his employees were Mexican. Many of them spoke English poorly. They understood Bill incompletely, and there were lots of misunderstandings, but they all had a good time of it and a lot of work got done.

Bill was sick all the time, but nobody gave it much thought because he was such a tough old bird. So they were all caught by surprise when he died suddenly of a heart attack on Tuesday morning. As the news spread through the restaurant and the kitchen, they became aware of how much they had cared for him and how much they would miss him.

On Wednesday afternoon Manuella, Bill's assistant, asked to speak to the owner. "Will we be given time off to go to Bill's funeral?" she asked.

"Yes," said the owner, "but it won't be a funeral exactly. Just a memorial service. The family wants the funeral to be private."

"Oh," said Manuella quietly. "Will he be there so we can say good-bye to him?"

"No," said the owner, "the casket won't be there."

"Can we visit the funeral home to say good-bye and tell his family how much we respected him?"

"No," responded the owner, "they would prefer to be left alone."

"I see," she replied. "Can we have a picture at the service so that we can say good-bye and tell him that we loved him?"

"Sure," said the owner.

"Will they tell us where he is buried so we can leave flowers on the grave?" she asked.

He told her they would.

"That will be nice," said Manuella.

This experience, which might have been painful to many people, was not to Manuella. She was speaking through a strong identity and a known set of cultural habits. She was firmly in touch with her covenant with life. Where she came from, you honor those who have died in a particular way. She had learned to do what it took to make this happen. Although the family's insult was not lost on her, it had no power to diminish her. Everyone has roots that can be uncovered and known, beliefs and gifts that ground us, providing direction when the temptation to forget who we are presses in on us.

## Establishing Inventive Groups

Eventually, if you stay on this transitional journey, an authentic internal voice becomes clearer and clearer, and you begin to make choices based on its calling. In the place of relentless confusion comes a sense that you are in a known territory that has familiar landmarks in it. There is room here for calm experimentation, for the emergence of diverse feelings and ideas. You can see and measure in this space, you can compare and know what is what. There is room here for you to move with grace and skill. It feels natural.

In this territory you begin to realize that regardless of what anyone else thinks, you can act authentically. You can respond wisely to problems that previously seemed not to have solutions. This discovery of your genuine being in the world is a discovery of where the power of life is generated. It is where the confidence and knowledge to make great changes come from.

But this confidence needs an ally. Most organizations cannot be counted on to embrace genuinely new ideas or authentic dialogues. So if these new discoveries are going to be nurtured, you need the forthright support of an inventive group—a philosophical work group (see Chapter Two) that comes together to solve problems. The world's great cities understood the role of inventive groups in fostering transition. They are known for the power they exercised in uncovering and strengthening the genius of a people. They attracted those who were exploring radically new ideas, offering them encouragement, information, and support. They provided a grounding so that people making the new efforts felt a continuity and security. These cities welcomed a confluence of people who regenerated life and developed new paradigms.

This is the pattern as well of great universities, scientific communities, and business labs.

These cities live in you metaphorically and in the work groups of inventive colleagues you have established. These groups must support your continuing discovery of who you are wherever it leads. *Wherever* it leads. When this happens, the benefits that flow to you and to the organization will be creative and practical. They may lead to great inventions or to wise accommodations—new creations free from the confusions of the daily drift.

> The personnel department at an East Coast financial institution was a battlefield. The company had responded chaotically to the deregulation that was changing the nature of the financial institutions across America, and the old way of doing business was dying a hard death. Bankers who had assumed for years that financial institutions needed to stand for solidity and stability were clashing with those who wanted to market new products and services. There was constant bloodletting and conflicting orders were flung about with regularity.
>
> The personnel department—nobody's idea of a cutting-edge force—got the washes of confusion secondhand. They were not in touch with the major combatants in the institution, so they were not consulted about matters that directly involved them. They were expected to do contradictory things by the many people who thought they were experts on what service the personnel department should provide the company.
>
> Having no outlet for creative energy, not empowered to devise their own solutions for broken-down systems, they snarled and bit at one another incessantly. When I sat down to work with them, my mission was modest—to calm the waters so that they could make it through the day a little better.

They began by clarifying the situation, listing the factors that were upsetting them. Then they classified the problems. First came those dealing with the many authority figures who made life unpleasant. They could not stop these rogue elephants from trampling around, of course, but they might be able to find a unified way of dealing with them. Right now they could not agree on the time of day, let alone how to handle the attacks that grew as the crisis thickened. So they decided to begin at home by unlocking the conflicts that kept them isolated from one another. They began to look frankly at what was not working among them, taking personal responsibility for coming out with their irritations and frustrations. If the bank was not able to get it together, the personnel department would.

Asked to write down and then communicate what wasn't working for them in their relations with their coworkers, they entered the stage of acknowledging that their own paradigm had broken down. Whatever the bank was doing wrong, they were adding to the problem. They were full of self-pity and were not taking responsibility for their own actions. This process of recognition affected them deeply. It did not make them less angry at the bank leaders, but it made them aware of their own sphere of influence. It gave their exploration a goal; they could make a difference here.

As they discussed what was not working in their relations with the others in the room, they all began to notice that they had the same kinds of struggles with everyone. Each of them had their own personal way of hurting and being hurt, and they began to suspect that they could construct a new way of handling conflict by taking personal responsibility for a small range of activities. They were trying it now and finding it effective.

Processes of this sort can backfire if they are not handled with great care. I was concerned in particular that it might be too much for one of the participants who had just emerged, two months earlier, from a psychiatric hospital. He was still a bundle of exposed nerve endings.

Imagine my consternation when the person who worked most closely with him did not let this slow her down a bit. When her time came to describe what was not working, she laid him out. "Ed, you go around acting as if you don't know your job. You act as if everything is a crisis, and it's not necessary. You know very well what you're doing. I wish you'd calm down." Ed was riveted. He looked at her for several minutes in silence. Then he said, "I know." I was standing by, eyes out on stalks, ready to reestablish a sense of safety in the event of a negative reaction, but it was not needed. People are often stronger than they appear.

Seeing this exchange, others began to take a deeper cut in their comments. As they did this, they began to notice that they mattered very much to one another even if that was revealed through occasional anger. As they expressed themselves and listened to the feedback they were getting, they sensed a healing of some frustrations, they encountered an ability to know and to manifest ideas, they began to feel more confident.

The next stage of the process was to uncover what strength they all had that had not been destroyed or violated by the depredations of everyday work life, reaching down to discover personal qualities that lived in them at a very basic level. They were asked to write down a list of the contributions they felt they made at work, to acknowledge what was unique about themselves, and then to make a similar list about everybody else in the room. After each person read his or her list out, acknowledging what they held as unique and valuable about themselves, everyone else took a turn at reading out the contributions that person made. In every case they found that others saw qualities they thought were not recognized, and they discovered others they had not listed that were widely perceived by their colleagues.

When Ed's turn came around he surprised himself by acknowledging that he knew he was competent and well trained. But this was just the first discovery. When Nora, who had been frighteningly direct with him earlier, finished reading out her list of his contributions she said, "There's something else, Ed. There's a word that always comes to mind when I think of you. It's friend. You're everything a friend should be. It's an honor to know you."

With this the walls of fear and isolation came crashing down and a new level of discourse began. Each person was acknowledged as having some unique qualities and strengths to offer. This was no longer a group of victims, but a group of people with obvious contributions to make. They had made a momentous discovery.

They used this new knowledge to generate an understanding of which problems they could respond to and which were out of their hands. They developed a set of guidelines for handling the problems they could and they came up with some stress-reducing methods for responding to those they could not change. (These involved strategies, policies, code names, symbols for when to retreat, and agreements on how to fend off some attacks.) As they came up with these ideas, gales of laughter swept the room; they were growing amused and occasionally delighted with the ideas they were generating. They agreed to meet once a month to monitor their results and to make up new methods to cope with the insults that their crazed company kept generating for them.

A year later the bank was still in trouble, but the personnel department had come to be known as an unusually inventive operation that was able to find unexpected solutions to difficult problems. Its members had come to see that they could express who they really were in the workplace, and that this process was gratifying and practical. And that it created power and respect.

## Making Your Contribution

One of the transforming aspects of discussing your unique contribution is that it changes your relationships. Acknowledging who you really are means you will play a role in leading the forces of transition, no matter where you are located in the organization. A successful leader has a vision that he or she is able to articulate in a way that attracts others. A newly compelling vision will have begun to emerge as you asked yourself the questions that make up the fifth practice. This vision will engage you, and your engagement will move others. Action is generated this way.

Your leadership will be manifested in part by a new openness and ease in working with others. You will begin to remove any obstacles you can that block peoples' capacity to invent. You will do this in the course of doing it for yourself. You will begin to create a work territory that is open and clear, where natural principles may be discovered that align you and your colleagues with powerful forces. No one style is necessary for the success of this sort of leadership. Some do it calmly and carefully, others are loud and blustery, still others are abrupt. The most effective change agents learn what they do best, what they enjoy, and what they have unusual energy for, and they build their style around that. You become a leader through this search process as surely as if you have been anointed. When you reach this stage, you no longer wait to be empowered by others, you empower them and through that process you earn power and credibility.

Times of transition produce new leaders who work together creatively, if not always harmoniously. The question that animates the most effective among them is not whether people are doing what the new leaders want them to, but rather are the leaders staying in contact with the things they value. Do they have the courage to listen to others and to search for what is needed regardless of the consequences? Will they tell people what they discover, and will they speak with the intention of being understood and listen with the intention of understanding?

## Showing Off for Lou

Leading the Southern branch of a Northern company was not an easy life. The executive committee was constantly frustrated. They felt they were never given the opportunity to provide input when sales and marketing strategies were being developed or when operational decisions were being made. The northerners looked down on them, did not take them seriously, were amused by their accents, assumed that they were less bright, less competent than they were. In this company regional operations in general had very little influence. The Southern office had even less.

The executive committee was resigned to this fate, although they resented it. They performed competently but listlessly; each of them did his or her job, then went home for the evening and spent their spare time arguing. They had some memorable disagreements.

The company wasn't setting the world on fire either, and the Northern leaders liked to blame regional leadership for their problems. When corporate officers visited the Southern region they came to sneer; those from the region sneered right back. These visits were painful and marked by acute anxiety. One day the boss came flying in, saw a report on overtime pay he did not like and went out of control. Slamming the department head against the wall, he made it clear

that this was not good enough and that it was never
to happen again. A lot of people saw the performance and
they were horrified. The department head was enraged.
"Lou called to apologize the next day, but it was too late. I
lost what respect I had for him that day and I just can't
get it back."

He and the other members of the executive committee
had long been biding their time, going through the motions.
The company was not a rewarding place to work; there was
no sense of accomplishment for them. The overtime attack
became a triggering event that signaled the collapse of their
belief in the company. Members of the executive committee
began to give voice to their doubts in weekly meetings, and
they began to feel frightened. They looked back at their
careers, looked at their future with the company. They began
to think about who they were and what they wanted out of
life; they began to discuss these questions of identity intensely. For a time they felt lost, and then something amazing
happened. They decided to act as if they actually had the
authority to make meaningful decisions, as if what they did
might make a difference.

They met to determine what their situation actually was:
What could they do to make up for shortfalls? What pieces
of bad news did they need to do something about and which
ones ignore? They began to think that a new product should
be developed, one that would sell in the South. They knew
that corporate would never let them do it—would not support the effort with development or marketing funds—but
they went ahead. "What did it matter?" said one of them.
"We had nothing to lose. It was sort of a personal thing."

They became corporate outlaws. Acting in violation
of their job descriptions and the unspoken boundaries of
authority, they had brainstorming sessions where ideas were

thrown around and written down. They began to explore possibilities. Each member of the committee contributed his or her expertise, noting what costs and benefits would accrue in each department. They chose the idea they liked best and did what research they could. They contacted suppliers, estimated costs, and developed a plan of attack.

And they built an internal strategy to gain acceptance. They notified friendly representatives from the corporate office that they were coming up with a product and would want a hearing. They set dates for previews and created opportunities for support. Amazed at this unprecedented activity, some people in corporate sat up and took notice. Two of them wanted to play and began to contribute advice and information.

None of them had done this before, but they stumbled along very well. It took long hours and extra work and they loved it. Their work sessions were wild, energetic, and funny, and only traces of the old rancorous melodrama were in evidence. They set a date for a preview presentation for their two allies from corporate office; they had never planned anything so well in their lives and it went off swimmingly. The idea was creative, appropriate for the company and the regional market, and the background information was well prepared. The two Northern representatives, one of them quite powerful, climbed enthusiastically onto the band wagon.

These representatives returned to corporate and primed the big guy. By the time he arrived for the final presentation two weeks later, he had told his lieutenants that he would act nice and say yes. The presentation, of course, was a success, and the Southern executive staff was overjoyed. Although they still did not like the boss any more than they had, he was still the big guy and succeeding with him was a thrill to them.

As they emerged from the meeting one of them said, "They say that living well is the best revenge and I believe it. Showing off for Lou was real nice."

The Southern leaders were not philosophers, but they had reached down, asked the hard questions, and found some basic truths. They discovered that they did not need to feel extinguished when they were ignored or even abused. As they recalled who they were, they realized that they could take some action, that they knew what would sell in their region, what products the company could produce, and how to make a focused proposal. They had more knowledge, power, and courage than they had expected.

And they learned how to enjoy themselves. Because what they did was outside the accepted bounds of their work, it began as extracurricular activity; it was playing. Playing can be an activity that opens people up to new possibilities. It is a way of being that makes the oppressions of the daily grind less central. When play and enjoyment join with practical projects, wonderful and unique results can occur. In this case the results would have seemed impossible a few months previously. Never in the company's history had the impetus for a new product emanated from a regional headquarters.

## Doing What You Do Best

Once you have discovered your unique contribution, you will gravitate to work that allows you to make it. I know a consultant who is a master of this art. Early in my career he hired me to work on a project he was doing at a California think tank. "What's the key to finding such perfect projects, Green?" I asked, excited by the quality of the work he had arranged. "Make them hire you to do what you do best," he responded.

I began to watch how he brought that feat off. Sitting in a meeting with clients, he would begin a dialogue about their problems. As the discussion progressed he looked for places where a need coincided with his best talents, zoomed in, and got more focused and intense. He threw out alternatives, made unexpected suggestions. He showed off. The clients got to hear a lot of in-depth knowledge, a point of view they had not considered, and what others in the field were doing. What he said was always unique and interesting and they almost always made a deal. The result was a series of brilliant projects.

That was his system for working with colleagues, too. As the weeks passed on the first project, I began to notice a pattern emerging that I had not expected, and I spoke to him about it. I said, "I'm beginning to make the assumption, Green, that the way we are going to do this is that you will come up with the brilliant ideas and I will do the research and analysis." "I adore that assumption," replied Green. So did I and so did the client, because there was plenty of room in it for all of us to have a good time with it. When you do what you do best, you can find other people to contribute what they do to fill in the spaces.

If you work in a job that does not call for your best, this is not so easy. But the practice of uncovering your unique contribution helps you discover how flexible you can be. You will discover that one part of your skill base is the ability to adjust to reality in a way that is usually creative and rewarding. This is true for organizations as well. An organization that moves according to this principle is constantly discovering resources it never knew it had.

Jeffrey's company was growing rapidly during the seventies. Once a family-held corporation, now it was going public.

The executive staff was reorganized, and so was the management structure. They upgraded their technology and diversified, but their big venture was buying a company that would get them involved in a new market. It was a mistake.

"This company was way out of our area of knowledge," said Jeffrey. "We didn't realize the scams they had been running in order to look good on paper. We thought that bringing our sense of efficiency to them would increase sales, but we ended up not being able to sell their products any better than they did. When that didn't work, we didn't know what was wrong and we didn't know how to diagnose the problem. We lost our ass."

Then they became smarter. They transferred their affections to another company they had started themselves. It was an adjunct to their traditional work and they knew this field well. Said Jeffrey, "This second company was a different story. We raised it from a pup and even though it took some time to develop, it was sound. We knew how to correct the mistakes we made along the way and now it's really taking off."

It worked so well that they sought other expansive activities that fell within their area of greatest knowledge. "We found a great one," said Jeffrey. "A huge corporation needed a product similar to our hottest item so we talked them into subcontracting with us for it. We can do that stuff in our sleep and it's effective for them because they were taking a beating trying to do it in house. Their hearts weren't really in it, so they kept inadvertently setting up procedures that cut off resources and made the process ineffective. But we do a great job and it makes us a nice profit."

When you do what you do best, real-world results—and that includes your feelings and energy level—leave no doubt about it.

You find yourself in action before you know it. Although you did not plan it, you have participated in a transformation, the creation of something genuinely new.

## The Final Steps of Transition

During this process of transition, you and the organizations you care about will be answering riddles, accepting challenges, undergoing unexplained ordeals, and encountering monsters and angels daily. For much of this time you will have felt humiliated that you cannot handle everything with aplomb. What a relief it is finally to discover that this fantasy of perfection is just another part of the learning process and that you can relax. You can begin to let some of the identities you have tried to assume, and the struggles that go with them, fall to the side.

Learning to express yourself—coming to know your real contribution and to enjoy making it—generates previously unimagined responses to significant problems. But it does more than that. Although we participate in transitions in order to survive, we do it also in order to flourish and to live meaningfully. We follow this road so that we may reveal ourselves in the world, so that we may be seen and may create something new that is our own contribution. In the process of discovering and manifesting who we are, we will shed many beliefs and some relationships that we have cared for, and this can be painful. But we have not given everything up. Our childhood dreams live in us more fully now; so do the dreams of those we love who are no longer here. So also do people and dreams we do not know yet, and we touch them now by responding to our own inner voice.

# 8

## Create Knowledge-Based Relationships

We have been talking about creating a particular state of mind in people who want to transform the organizations they care about. This state of mind is characterized by a mental clarity, an openness to new information, and an ability to make effective adjustments to emerging conditions. It is a way of perceiving and inventing that brings a person into direct contact with the laws of nature and the marketplace.

But creating an organization that can respond authentically to the world cannot be done in your mind nor can it be done alone. If you are interested in creating regeneration, you need to develop relationships that foster the growth of self-knowledge in the whole organization. These relationships will restructure the foundations of power and lead to action. During times of transition, choosing to be effective means forming these knowledge-based relationships.

Consequently, at this point change agents need to turn their attention from practices that focus on personal discovery to those that transform the perceptions and activities of the whole organization. Knowledge-based relationships, partnerships, and alliances that foster awareness, self-knowledge, and action will be the foundation of that work.

## Getting Started

I will assume that you have read this book carefully so far, that you have worked at all the practices, called your friends, and written postcards to acquaintances to tell them about it. Your life has turned around and your warts have all cleared up.

You are soaring with self-discovery, in touch with your deeper self and the world, creative as never before, interesting to people who used to think of you as boring. Wherever you go people are saying how wonderful it all is. And you say, "Do you really think so? That's great. Let's do this for the whole organization. Think what we can accomplish."

They love it. They say, "You bet. Let's do it." But they probably are not going to do a thing, and getting angry about it is useless. Most of them *want to want* it to happen. Some of them *do* want it to happen, but when it is time for action most people do not intend to do anything.

> I walked into the CEO's office and before me was a magnificent view. New Jersey woodlands stretched out as far as we could see. Beautiful furniture and artwork were everywhere and the feeling of carefully manifested good taste was strong. This was the result of time and hard work, and attention to detail.
>
> The CEO spoke of the emerging needs of his growing organization: its new management system and how important it was to integrate it successfully into the old culture, the new technology that was revolutionizing the

sales and warehousing functions, the new marketing concept, and the new sense of partnership with employees. His
discussion of these ideas was as thoughtful and tasteful as his
office decoration. And it was no more likely to make any
difference to his company's turnaround efforts than the
paintings were. He talked a wonderful game, but my experiences over the next few weeks made it clear that he was
committed to taking no new action.

He was overwhelmed. All the growth had outstripped
the staff's ability to measure, predict, and act. The company
had entered some new markets and the results were not what
had been expected. Staff had been added haphazardly as new
needs emerged, and it was getting expensive. The new technology was loaded with problems, and the staff was unsure
who to believe when the experts gave conflicting advice.

This was not his father's Oldsmobile and he was getting
very frightened. He knew that the company had lost money
last year, but the accountants had not told him how much
yet, and he was in no hurry to find out because he did not
know what to do about it. He was in no hurry, that is, until
the bank began to get urgent about loans.

Was this a time to do more than talk artfully about the
new age of business? Should he begin to plan drastic new
approaches, reject the old way of working? He thought not,
but kept this unfashionable thought to himself. So he talked
like a figure out of the journals, uttering the new buzzwords,
gesturing deftly but, as he revealed later, feeling hollow and
frightened.

This dilemma is common today. People in the throes of crisis are
being asked by people like me to add considerably to their inse-
curity, to begin to explore who they are and what they stand for. I
am not surprised that many find this difficult and prefer to talk

big talk. The nature of the problem they face, that we all face if we want to begin constructing organizations that are in touch with reality, is significant.

Most organizations are inherently resistant to transition. Their leaders get where they are because they are able to maintain a stabilizing culture. It is the culture and not nature they stay in touch with. They become convinced that this, not transformation, is the road to survival. Most of the people working in the structure believe this, too. The collapse of an old system does not dislodge people from belief in it. It often increases their loyalty.

The concept of cognitive dissonance suggests that people who see a distressing disparity between what they believe and the way the world works tend to become more attached to the old belief. The more events seem to disprove it, the more firmly the belief is defended. And those who have the most intense relationship to this belief, those who have sacrificed much or are paid well for their compliance, will be the fiercest adherents. This behavior has been observed repeatedly by researchers who systematically study people working in situations where change is hot and heavy. Startling at first, it has been corroborated repeatedly and has become a response that is expected by organization development professionals.

To bring an organization into a new alignment with reality, plan on dealing with all these defensive phenomena. Expect denial, resistance, and sabotage. Expect grudging compliance rather than committed action. Decide that you would not have it any other way, because these responses are natural. They are a part of the natural laws you are seeking to understand. Learn how to work with these forces and not against them.

The key to success is not whether or not other people resist, but the integrity with which you pursue this strategy. Are you disciplined without being rigid? Are you honest and responsible?

Are you fully engaged? Are you giving it your best? Are you communicating effectively and making decisions when they are appropriate? If you do not mean it, if you get sloppy or are content to blame others for not doing what you think they should, you will fail. And you will spend lots of valuable energy looking for scapegoats.

No matter how ably you do this work, circumspection is wise in determining what to promise when you undertake it. People will want to be assured that you will turn the organization around or make it quick money, and you cannot in good faith promise that. You can, however, promise that if they get in and play hard, they will produce a new mind set, a new basis for creating intellectual capital. You can tell them that the possibility exists for the creation of a transformed organization that is at home and effective in the emerging world, but that nobody can guarantee this result. That possibility will not sound like enough to many leaders who are beset by crisis. It sounds too vague and intangible, but it is the best you can offer. Even the most effective change programs tend to end before they are complete.

Yet undertaking the task is wonderful work. It gives birth to great creations, stops decline, and begins the work of rebuilding. It is a road to the fullest deployment of the human gift and one of the primary reasons we create organizations.

## Forming Effective Partnerships

Transition means restructuring the foundations of power. So if you are interested in creating regeneration, you need to build a firm power base. You need to create effective partnerships that are driven by a goal big enough to encompass the interests of everyone. During times of transition, choosing to lead means to form partnerships.

Power in organizations that are changing begins to float free of hierarchical position and relationships that produce new influence become very important. These relationships are built on information, insight, knowledge of what is going on, and an ability to see connections between events. The skills it takes to gather these resources are not necessarily those practiced by the people at the top.

Leaders of transition will emerge from many places in the structure and they must move deftly. Bold action is often a good idea, but making raids on other peoples' connections, resources, and information sources will not regenerate anything. Offending unnecessarily is foolish. There will have been considerable coercive power flowing through the arteries of the organization as it suffers the disintegration of the old arrangements. What is needed now is new legitimacy, so if you are interested in leading from the ranks, you must model the creative and collaborative behavior that will become the standard. If you are the leader already, you are wise to bring the people who report to you to choose you again because of your ability to form effective relationships.

The first phase of this work is to begin to form knowledge-based partnerships—formal or informal relationships that are designed to achieve specific goals—with people outside your work group. The goal of these relationships is to discover what is really happening and what is genuinely possible. This is not likely to be the foundation of your old relationships, so you will need to build new ones consciously and carefully. The natural candidates are people who share goals and functions with you. You will have worked with them often, but now you will be approaching them in a slightly new way. Here are some guidelines for these activities:

• Start with a project you both understand and to which you are both committed. Decide what result you want, and communicate it with the intention of being understood. Come right out of hiding and say it. Be specific in your requests, and make them reasonable. If, as you move along, you feel that what you want needs to change, say so and communicate that clearly.

• Listen to what the other person wants. Committed listening is the key to enrollment. If you want a real partner when the shooting starts, you need to be sure that there is something deeply rewarding for them in this relationship. When you and your partner both do this, you end up enrolling each other in a new project that is born through this interaction. It will not be exactly what either of you wanted when you began. In fact, if you have gotten exactly what you started out wanting, you probably have not reached a real agreement.

• Define this new agreement well. It is the starting point for action. Set goals and rules.

• Bring all of yourself to this activity. Imagine, visualize, create, plan, be an individual. Brainstorm, give support, and accept it. If you are not enjoying this, do something you like. This is a way of living, not a tactic.

• Expect breakdowns. Misunderstanding, sabotage, failure, and fatigue are natural parts of the process. Notice, in particular, the ways you have of gesturing and not entirely doing what it takes to succeed. We all do this. Know when this happens that it is not someone's fault.

• Expect breakthroughs. That is what you are here to create. You *can* teach an old dog new tricks. History is nothing if it is not the story of old dogs dancing to new tunes.

• Take responsibility for the success of this partnership and its goals. Ground your efforts in time and space. Create agreed-on activities with boundaries and deadlines. Measure results and check in often.

• Seek feedback. Listen to your results and notice how people respond to you. Set new goals based on what has worked and what has not. Take new ground.

• Pace yourself. This work does not go smoothly, nor does it create optimal value if it is a product of incessant pressure. Do not let the author of a book, someone you probably never met, encourage you to run around being frantic.

## Deciding to Go for It

If you have followed the six practices, you have grown used to having your word mean something in your work group. You will have done the difficult work of trying and failing to understand yourself in action, you will have heard the feedback, shifted, and got better at it, crashed again, got up, and gone after it until finally a coherence begins to appear between word and deed. After that you will understand the vicissitudes of this process, and you will know this discipline when it arises in the larger organization. You will not be distressed when success is followed by a setback, or astounded when a major advance seems to come from nowhere. You will not feel like a rag doll thrown around at will, a prey to forces you do not understand.

If, as the real magnitude of this work becomes more evident, you realize that you do not want to do it, you can get clear on what you actually do want. A real vision is what moves you, not what moved the author of an article or a workshop trainer, or your parents or colleagues. Looking at what you really want may frighten you if you suspect that it is not what you should want, but if you refuse to take a look at this situation, and stay asleep in order to ignore it, you are in for big trouble. And looking at your genuine motivation in the situation is the key to producing gratifying responses to difficult situations.

Rachel inherited a company. It had come as a surprise. Her parents wanted to keep it in the family, but neither of her older brothers would have anything to do with it. She agreed to work for her father for a year after graduate school while she figured out what she wanted to do, and although it was not her intention to stay, she did so well that the stopping point never seemed to arrive.

Seven years later, she was not as interested as she felt she should be. She was getting tired of it, the marketplace was changing, and her caretaker role was no longer enough. She had been hiding from the evidence, and she began to spend a lot of time away from work, traveling and collecting antiques. Although she was conscientious, her heart was not in the business. Things were getting to be a mess.

The crisis began to surface and she allowed herself to be convinced that she needed to look at the situation with clarity. She and several advisors gathered information on how the company was doing. Little by little it became clear that if they continued as they were, the future was not bright. They had begun to make their money on products she considered collateral, while the main activities, those her father had developed, were costing them big bucks. As she and her advisors looked into the implications of this, the effort it would take—both the technical work and the people work—to bring coherence and a bright future to the company overwhelmed her.

Plan after plan was developed, strategy after strategy was explored and the thought of them exhausted her. But the process served her well. Slowly, two ideas began to dawn on her. The first was that her interests were elsewhere, that she really did not want to do this. Staying on to do a halfway job would be irresponsible. The second realization was that she could hire someone else to do it for her. She could bring in someone who wanted to do this, who was trained for it, and whose chances of success were strong.

She began to look closely at this possibility. She checked it out from every angle. First she explored her own interests more fully and made some gratifying decisions about how she would spend her time in the future. This excited her and gave her the energy to pursue the transition. Then she put together a brain trust that helped her determine the guidelines for the new company and criteria for the new leader's selection. In time, that leader was chosen and a well-structured relationship was designed between him and her. She reduced her activities over the period of a year while remaining in touch in a way that worked for everyone involved.

She has a well-defined role, particularly in determining policy, and she has more accurate information than she ever did. The new team directs daily operations; they have broad authority to invent and implement. Employees are getting guidance, setting practical goals, and feeling that they are part of an organization with a mission and a future. Occasionally she gets crazy about something or other and intervenes in a way that seriously upsets the new leadership, but the situation is dramatically better than it was. Rachel and a whole lot of people in the company are much happier now.

Not many of us have the luxury of the choice that Rachel did. It took plenty of guts for her to do it, however, and her ultimate success was grounded in the fact that her strategy grew out of a knowledge-based relationship with her advisors and eventually the whole company. She stopped kidding herself, then she stopped kidding them. The result was that everybody got an opportunity to take sensible action. It was no easier for her employees to do this than it was for her. Being right about the dangers of her procrastination had not required great perceptive skill or courage, but deciding to respond effectively to the new opportunity she created was a challenge to them.

## Creating the Context

If I were approaching a potential transitional leader at a cocktail party to offer my best advice, much as the old man approached Dustin Hoffman in *The Graduate*, I would not whisper "plastics" as he did. I would whisper "context." When the foundation for what you do is a context that is understood by others, and to some extent shared by them, the chances for success multiply greatly.

This requirement is more complex than it first appears. It implies that you are willing to be open about your goals and methods, that others may inquire into your motives without evoking mad revenge on your part, and that you are willing to have your words compared to your actions. You do not have to run around sprouting a halo to succeed at this, but you are wise to be reasonably accountable. This may seem extreme, but if you have been working on a set of practices that increase your self-awareness, you will see this as an opportunity to express yourself (as well as a steep requirement).

Another reason for setting the context is that people are put at ease when they understand what you are up to, even if they do not like it. They are more receptive to hearing your point of view, more open to collaboration. When you make proposals or suggest strategies or rules, your chances of emerging with an agreement are strengthened. You are building legitimacy.

This legitimacy, however, requires vigilance. It means moving toward results that bring benefits to the whole organization.

It implies that you are inviting others to express their needs and those of the organization and that you will respond to these expressions. If in your zeal to produce a new dawning you run all over people, you will trample legitimacy and re-create the old relationships to power that have not been working.

Mike is a no-nonsense manager. He is energetic, tough, and full of great ideas, and when he joined the management team at a new company, he was excited by his charge. He was to be part of a turnaround, one that was badly needed and anxiously awaited by the employees. This was the opportunity of a lifetime. Here he could really make a difference. There would be a small team, six of them, who would direct this effort. Six good people. Six experienced professionals.

He spent his first months scouting the place out and planning his strategy. Then he jumped into action. He reorganized his department, brought in some better technology, and took the reins into his hands. He would brook no opposition, but he was open and friendly. Although he asked others to make a major effort, nobody worked as hard as Mike did.

One day, in the course of several major projects, he wrote a memo that seemed unimportant, but that was to cause him trouble. Previously all employees had been able to park wherever they wanted to in the parking lot. Mike put a stop to it. "Park only in the farthest lot," he told them. "Customers need to park near the building." Only the executive committee, he decreed, could continue to park anywhere.

This made him an unpopular man. Within hours of the memo's appearance, a furor had been whipped up.

Expressions of indignation were made, a petition was started, his phone began to ring. People were angry, and, most surprising to Mike, some of the angriest were department heads who should know better. What was going on?

What Mike did not know was that not long before his arrival the department heads, all twelve of them, had reported to the sectional vice president. They were the decision-making body for the place. A streamlining plan had reduced this twelve-member board to the present six-person executive committee. The other six people felt shafted. When these people saw that parking-lot insult was to be added to this earlier injury, they vented their wrath on Mike.

Because what he had done was perfectly reasonable, Mike held his ground and got to be known as inflexible. Mike got madder by the minute; he felt isolated as this affair became a symbol for many events that had annoyed people for years. It took a surprisingly long time for Mike to work his way out of this, and while he was doing it, many of his projects were not seen as legitimate by people whose cooperation he badly needed.

If Mike had asked around, he would have been told about the background and then he could have set a context for the memo. He could have lined up some support and found a way to do it that would have been understood. It would have taken more time than dashing off the memo had, but it would have saved months of trouble.

If he had been genuinely interested in constructing effective partnerships, he would not have been such a ready target for misunderstanding. Mike is a good guy who will do anything for a friend, who supports employees, rolls up his sleeves to work with them, and who genuinely cares for them. They discovered this pretty soon, too. But being a good guy is not the same as being perceived as a legitimate leader. Not even close.

If he had dipped into his Plato, Mike would have known that since ancient times it has been considered appropriate for every law to have a preamble, a statement that walks before it, justifying and explaining. Such a context creates a pace and a movement that are congenial to people, showing them a face of awareness, one that cares that they know and understand.

To create effective results during times of transition you must be awake, alert, and in touch with the context. Take a good look around, respect sensibilities, and watch the boundaries. When you see people hovering about, looking worried and upset, listen to their concerns, increase the circle of understanding around your projects, and support others in their projects.

Building legitimate power can only happen after you understand the culture you are in and ground your activities in the values of the community. It is from this community that support, resources, and power come during transition. It determines what plans will be successfully implemented and which ones will not. Building power here means demonstrating that you want success for others in the organization. This is not the same as liking them. Transitional power bases are built on shared goals and honesty more than on personal affection.

Bruce is opinionated and not bashful about expressing himself. Nobody doubts where he stands on issues or people. But when the action gets intense, he becomes direct and available to anyone who is important to the success of the project at hand. His personal feelings about them are dropped to an extent that is amazing.

There is one vice president, however, who tries Bruce's patience gravely. Bruce feels that this man is not entirely ethical, that he is far from accurate in his work, and not to be trusted. Yet they worked remarkably well on a major project, and Bruce never once complained about him. I thought they had learned to like one another.

When the project was successfully completed, the vice president went off on a well-earned fancy vacation. He returned two weeks later tanned, trim, and impeccably dressed. Hearing that the man had returned, I called Bruce to see if they were still pals now that the crisis had passed. "How was Cal today," I asked. "Gleaming like a ruby in a goat's ass," he replied.

If you can only work with people you like, or who like you, your range of effectiveness is drastically limited. Powerful partnerships and work teams often bring together people who would not normally give each other the time of day. What matters is your capacity for coordinated action, not personal affection. What works is to keep your professional focus on the goal and your personal focus on knowing yourself.

Understanding how you can be effective, how you go into re-action, how you can get back on track—matters you have been engaged in with the first five practices—will create movement. Fascination with the perfidy of others is one of the ways you have been blocking yourself for years. Unless you are in the presence of legendary vileness, you will need to learn how to work with people you do not like or understand. Just do not invite them to your birthday party.

Building legitimate power eventually means to establish a cluster of working assumptions among people that facilitates growth and regeneration. These assumptions include a host of sentiments: I want what is best for myself and for others; I will do what it takes; I expect that others want what is best for me. These assumptions are not so much reflections of any existing reality as they are an assertion about how to proceed. They have to do with risk and trust and strength, not naïveté.

If you expect others to want this state of affairs, you will express your wishes clearly, appropriately, and compellingly. And not as a victim does, not in a way that will lead to a no or to confusion so that you can be right about how hopeless it all is, but forcefully and compellingly.

## Developing Alliances

Working with people who do not entirely share your goals, people who have some different interests, is essential to forming the alliances that produce transitions. Allies have their own constituencies to consider and while they seek partners who share common goals, they understand that their interests will not perfectly coincide. They expect a certain tension and independent action from one another and they do not get crazy when others fail to do everything they would like them to do.

This cluster of assumptions and activities generates power. It leads to the creation of common goals, new work rules, a shared strategy that is broad enough to encompass great amounts of useful information, and results that produce resources for many people. Talented and energetic people are commonly attracted to this because one of the resources that is most prized during transition is to be involved in the creation of the new culture. An alliance will design the new culture and wise people know that.

Knowledge-based relationships of this sort are formidable for another reason. They incorporate the knowledge of how to maintain a partnership during breakdown. Anyone can form partnerships when things are just fine. But that is not the territory of discovery and transition.

Because these activities are so powerful, they will attract the opposition of important people. And since the setting is transition, confusion and uncertainty will swirl around them. Your ability to maintain effective partnerships will depend upon your capacity to work well when you are uncertain, frightened, and annoyed. This activity takes courage and self-confidence and the wise use of all the skills you have been developing in order to stay afloat and enjoy it all.

## No More Mister Nice Guy

I once worked with a leader whose organization was badly out of whack. He knew that it needed a major overhaul, but he was not the sort who leads turnarounds. He was addicted to being a nice guy; seemed to be a terminal case. He never said anything unpleasant, seldom took a stand, and manipulated as much as he could in private. But the crisis affected him deeply, and he began learning how to construct legitimate power. Amazingly, he built one of the best alliance systems I have ever seen.

In a distressed organization, amidst storms of dissent and confusion, this Nice Guy rose like a phoenix. He met with his department heads and laid out his goals, expectations, and requests. They saw a clarity and strength in him about which they previously had not known. They responded to him in kind and feverish negotiation ensued.

Then, and this is crucial, they met as a group and everyone revealed the nature and details of their agreements to one another. They asked everyone in the room to consider each agreement carefully, to determine whether or not they would in good faith support this agreement. And, of course, new adjustments had to be made. Massive amounts of information had been exchanged; people had set goals and pledged time and resources.

Everyone was exposed. Other peoples' agreements are never a matter of indifference to those who must share goals and resources with one another.

And although problems arise in such a procedure, the nasty private skirmishes during which people do each other secret wrongs are more difficult in this setting. Agreements take on the nature of a public pledge. People build trust, legitimacy, and effective partnerships often when they only partly intend to. They get impressed with themselves and with the team. They create a transition before their very eyes. That is what happened to the Nice Guy and his staff.

But there is more. He required that each department head call in his or her lieutenants and get their approval before offering that department's services. As a result people in the departments knew a whole lot that they hadn't known before. They had more information. They had an opportunity to be honest with each other and to share some goals. It is difficult to show up as shortsighted or stingy in this system. Confidence and trust are engendered.

During this engagement the Nice Guy took off and soared; he became another hero for our time. At the end of the final meeting, when his staff had forged their hard-won agreements, he served them all champagne. They were flushed with excitement, brimming with confidence, aware that the road ahead was going to be difficult, but glad they had a strong team. He could not have been more impressive if he had emerged from a phone booth in tights and a cape.

Partnerships and alliances such as this are the heirs to the classic regenerating relationships of history. As they develop over time, they become similar to heroic friendships that are intimate but directed outward. They move people from unnecessary conflict with their own best interests and into action. After Parzival jousts unknowingly with his brother, his brother says, "On this field you were fighting with yourself. I came riding to battle with myself and would gladly have slain myself."

These are not friendships that seek buddyhood in order to make the rest of the world wrong; they are the direct recognition of another's human worth. This recognition is based on action and animated by the need to discover underlying principles and a determination to work with those principles in order to create something new. These relationships seek something that has not been before, not imagined or planned for, something that is brought into being through action in alignment with natural laws.

## The Rewards of Knowledge-Based Groups

These knowledge-based relationships are the foundation of inventive and nurturing groups. The process of growth in the group will be like the personal process we have been discussing. It must be given time, understanding, and care. It must be tempered and given real challenges to meet. Its progress will be uneven and fitful and it will seem odd and frightening at first. But it will eventually produce an alert engagement with reality so that opportunities worth grabbing get grabbed and problems are seen and handled as they develop.

The people in these groups will maintain an openness to the laws of nature rather than to the old culture's norms, and their interaction will be a kind of intimacy and vulnerability, not weakness or innocence. This means being vulnerable to your vision. As humans we are always vulnerable; that is part of the arrangement as Gilgamesh discovered, and we do not get to vote on it. We cannot change this—not through suffering, not through greatness. Gilgamesh discovered this, too. But we can choose some of the forces to which we are vulnerable. Integration and wholeness happen when we step outside ourselves and become part of expansive relationships. Here we reveal ourselves responding to life in a context where our best may be recognized for what it is. This is virtuosity and it is a great triumph.

These relationships always create new resources for the community and expand the allies' connections with the world. Yet what they set out to do is seldom the result they produce. In creating something new and unimagined, Gilgamesh and Enkidu set out to do what heroes do: slay a monster here, overcome a natural disaster there, work hard, fight bravely, and bring riches back to the city. The gods and goddesses must have winked at one another.

The end was something else altogether. It was the eventual recognition of the human condition, knowing the inevitability of death yet coming to see the regenerative power in human life, understanding consciously for the first time that human community is constantly being reborn through the living of everyday life. They could not possibly have thought that up in advance. It was not what they imagined and it was not what they wanted. What a magnificent gift.

# III

---

# Enduring Value

---

# 9

## The Awful Truth
## About Change

When you come into an organization determined to create a dynamic of human growth as the foundation for new effectiveness, people are likely to start growing. They will experience moments of maturity and strength and moments of wild confusion. They will be joyful one minute and furious the next. They will behave like adolescents.

Asked for their input when they are not used to being listened to, they can be angry and resentful. They are angry at you for asking in the first place and getting their hopes up when they know it will not do any good, and resentful that they are in this situation and that it is being pointed out to them. And then a very interesting phenomenon often occurs.

When employees who have had the lid screwed down hard are allowed to participate in committees that will set up new procedures, they often use the opportunity to attack one another. It is unusual for them to devise standards that give them more freedom or authority. They are more likely to focus on making up rules that get their least favorite coworkers good, just as they have been gotten.

Left to their own devices, these committees will address themselves to matters such as dress code, who may park their cars where, and when off-duty employees may come into the workplace. A favorite target at these times are other employees who seem to get away with not obeying unpopular rules.

These people are continuing to play according to the rules of the old system that at this stage is still very much intact. Organizations in transition tend to favor posturing over the honest pursuit of goals. They talk a lot about staff empowerment without actually attempting it, so the first efforts to turn this all around will seem like another gesture to employees. They play what appears to be the only game in town. They fake it.

In one situation, a manager who loved to look at herself had a mirror on the wall facing her desk so that this pleasant activity would be easy for her. She got clobbered by the first task force set up by a transitional management team. It was her short skirts that incensed some of her colleagues. They spoke forcefully in their first draft of an employee handbook about women who wore short skirts on the job. They did not want to get rid of rules that made their jobs more difficult or ask for more resources or improved working conditions. They wanted to get this floozy.

Just like their bosses, they do not know what taking responsibility in a new way might look like, so they mimic it and get lost in dramatic struggles over minor issues. This is nothing new. In ancient Greece, Aristophanes noted that conquering armies tended to make up laws for the defeated that read like drinking songs. We are still at it. This is typical human behavior, and if we want to move through this phase and into creative reconstruction during transitional periods, we need to have compassion for ourselves, our cohorts, and our bosses.

## Leaders in Distress

Why don't people jump for joy when reform comes to them and set about making immediate utopias? The answer by now is obvious. The organizational dynamics that build entrenched resistance to new and good things are similar to the personal dynamics we have been working to overcome in the six practices.

When old paradigms slowly disintegrate in their capacity to solve problems adequately, leaders find it difficult to get the results they expect. Then forms of coercion increasingly replace genuine engagement, and false sentiment masquerades as commitment. Both leaders and followers experience a shift of focus away from producing products and services and toward doing what they think is expected of them. Keeping the system going at all costs becomes everybody's primary concern, and since the system is less effective at solving problems than it once was, these two activities often are incongruent.

As this system protecting focus grows in importance, people become progressively disengaged from the stated goals of the organization and more attached to protecting its routines. A remarkably small percentage of the work day is spent producing products and services when this is true, yet people leave the office tense and worn out.

This becomes a chronic crisis that turns employees into observers whose primary interest is in pleasing those who are central to organizational discipline, to leaders or their spies. These observers pretend to be in action when it comes to meeting real world goals, but confusion runs rampant because those goals have become unreal and unattainable. People in such a system get to be good at looking as if they are busy while being unproductive. When you think of this, the people who spring to mind may be those you come into contact with when you are a client or customer (clerks, secretaries, waitresses, and the like). Some of them perform these acts of grudging compliance daily. Often with great crust.

A friend of mine is a keen observer of this phenomenon. His office overlooks a large work area. One employee who apparently does not realize that he can see her from his vantage point works furiously whenever he passes by. But when not aware that she is being observed, she seems to spend most of her time chewing away madly at great wads of gum. When she is lost in this activity, nothing else seems to matter, and she gives herself over to it body and soul. Pointing her out to me one day, he remarked, "I wonder who taught that woman to chew gum. I hope he also left her a trust fund."

But the most dangerous perpetrators of this fraud are the people at the top who say they want things to work better but who do not take action. These are the leaders who take stabs at setting new goals, changing the way things are done, and developing quality standards without following through. Theirs is the land of the easy vision statement that seems to fool them alone. Leaders who do not really mean it or do not understand the magnitude of this work get themselves into trouble.

When the prevailing paradigm is under stress in a workplace, force has increasingly replaced internalized belief and great whopping fantasies are supported by conspiracies of silence. Coercion masquerades as unity and employees are treated like children. They are seen as little folks who do not have the resources necessary to get the job done on their own. They are thought of as unlikely to work hard enough if not watched constantly, as incapable of solving problems, as only interested in themselves and unconcerned about the company's interests. Workers in this sort of setting are dependent and expected to screw up. And they do. Treated like children in the workplace, the most competent parent, complexly skilled friend, talented technician, or master of information will act like a child.

Leadership in an organization of this sort is also characterized by qualities that seem childish. Leaders tend to act capricious, impulsive, and irrational. The question they increasingly ask is not what can we do to meet the demands of the marketplace, but who can we blame for our problems. Nor is this surprising. Leaders are particularly vulnerable when the old ideas are losing their power. They are responsible for results that are becoming progressively more difficult to produce. The way of doing things they were taught is maddeningly ineffective. Their work methods are being questioned, and the beliefs and institutions that fortified them in the past are in trouble.

Because there are so few understandable external guidelines during these times, leaders' decisions and behavior are often driven by their moods. Discipline is random and difficult to predict. It is not uncommon for managers to tell frightened employees to humor the boss, pretend to listen to the tirades, nod the head, take a few notes, and then continue doing what they were before the episode began. Under these circumstances what matters most to workers is not goals, but handling these eruptions. Productivity suffers, and so does quality. So does self-respect.

These systems grow increasingly self-absorbed. They become severely restricted information fields where everything is perceived in the same rigid fashion and anything that contradicts the status quo is systematically ignored. Great amounts of information are not received and processed. The marketplace can change drastically, and the competition can metamorphose, and neither will be noticed nor responded to. These organizations bear an uncanny resemblance to our own fortresses and our own little soldiers. When we get righteous about a leader's irrationality, we usually do it from inside our fortresses, and we send our soldiers out to deal with it.

Not knowing what to do or how to measure results promotes learned helplessness and mental confusion in an organization. Timing is off; work is either very slow and deliberate, rushed and confused, or both. Many employees react passively. They dull themselves out. Their responses are characterized by lassitude, suppressed anger, and a search for scapegoats. They entertain unpleasant views of their own abilities and motivations. They do not trust their own senses, respect their own interests, or value their own perceptions about what is happening. They are sluggish and often unconsciously engaged in covert sabotage (doing work sloppily, calling in sick, being late, fighting unnecessary territorial disputes, agreeing to do things they have no intention of doing). It is not pretty.

## Trickle-Down Resistance

Even when this state of affairs grows abusive, many employees seem to accept it. One department head approached me to point out that he did not mind it when the boss used racial epithets against him. He took it, he said, as a sign of affection. Another was never more fiercely loyal than when she had been savaged by her boss. She would emerge from his office red faced but full of praise for him. In systems such as this, some people will protect the boss at all costs. If you set out to relieve them of what appears to be oppression, they are likely to respond with anger. It is naive to expect any other response, and it is a warning that you are intervening clumsily in a complex relationship.

This dynamic translates down through the system. There will be outbreaks of emotional violence that have uncanny repercussions. Events occurring at the top of the structure will be repeated at every level, even if the big guys are clobbering each other in secret. Workers do not need to see it to know about it. They carry the whole show inside themselves.

In one situation great stress led a department head to slap another department head. Although it happened in private, it caused a furor. For weeks relations were strained and lightning flashes of anger were discharged throughout the place. Several weeks later during a meeting I was holding with people working in the typing pool, a supervisor who reported to the slapping boss told of her difficulties in training a newcomer. The new person had talked back to her, had been rude, had embarrassed her. "What did you do?" I asked. She told of trying to explain in new ways, of persisting and not getting very far. Finally, she reported just walking away. "What did you want to do?" I asked in well-modulated tones. "I wanted to hit the bitch," she responded, to screams of delight from the others in the meeting.

Does this set of circumstances sound horrible? I hope not. I am not describing particularly unusual organizations. You do not have to be broken down for this to be true. It is common during transitions.

## The Characteristics of Transitional Organizations

A number of characteristics are prominent in the behavior of people in transitional organizations. Most of them are basic human qualities, but at times of crisis these qualities become particularly important. They take on the power to block effective work and creative responses to new possibilities. Recognizing the characteristics is useful if you want to react wisely to them. They include:

• Being right. People feel that being wrong or incorrect is especially dangerous. They will go to great extremes to prove that they are right about the smallest matters. Being wrong brings on punishment from above and an isolating withdrawal on the part of colleagues. This blocks curiosity, the search for new information, and creativity.

• Abandonment. The leader feels abandoned by the old ideas, by cohorts and employees. The organization, in turn, appears to have abandoned its people; secrets are kept, but promises are not. Meaningful personal contact is lost while gestures proliferate. And, most distressingly, nobody knows who to hold responsible for anything. Events seem mysterious and huge.

• Alienation. A particularly virulent variety of alienation is experienced; people become the object of their own contempt. Although this is often an unconscious feeling, it is corrosive and destructive. Forced repeatedly to express emotions that are unnatural, to do work that they resent, to pretend not to know what they know, to become increasingly distrustful of their own perceptions, people find that their self-respect and their identities are damaged.

• The fear of being found out. People entertain the suspicion that whoever they really are is not good enough. This crushes imagination and risk taking, qualities necessary for regeneration. People learn to control their feelings and behavior. Perfection, which is impossible, is sought with the result that plans, strategies, and actions are designed to avoid negative outcomes rather than to produce the most positive result.

An organization plagued with these characteristics inevitably experiences an identity crisis. It does not know what it is here for or what to do next. Its members are addicted to its dysfunctions. They behave like people who are so uncertain of themselves that they find their happiness and validation only in others, not in themselves or in their results. Alert action and productivity grind to a halt.

I do not want to be too dramatic about this. These characteristics are a given of the human experience. Learning to acknowledge that and not feel victimized by it is a primary goal of the search for self-knowledge. Yet these qualities run amok in organizations that get stuck in the process of making a transition. And the results can be devastating.

These dysfunctions, however, are only a symptom of the underlying problems. Creating a healthy response to them means to dig deeper and ask why all this seemingly crazy stuff happens so often?

It happens because by the time an organization gets stuck in the process of moving away from a malfunctioning paradigm, a number of basic elements have gotten out of alignment. This misalignment is a natural by-product of the march of time through any group's culture. Like an earthquake, crisis will come to the surface when certain essential factors have moved enough to become disjointed. Those factors are legitimacy, power, and community.

## The Role of Legitimacy

Legitimacy is an abstract idea with very serious practical consequences. It is a concept that has to do with definitions. It defines us as individuals; it defines our organizations and our culture. It sets boundaries and tells us who fits in and who does not. It says what you have to be and do in order to belong to a group and to lead it. It also defines how followers should behave, delineating their rights and duties.

When legitimacy is not working well, trust in leaders and institutions is shaken. It is difficult for us to know who we are and to feel confident about our organizations. Order and responsibility are undermined and obedience becomes a matter of unthinking habit, or of expediency or necessity. It is devoid of reason or principle; it is low on genuine sentiment and conviction. One does what one must, perhaps remaining defensively loyal to the prevailing order, but uneasy and edgy.

This has happened repeatedly in human history and it is happening now. It is epidemic in a modern world where it is unclear who makes decisions or according to what standards. Nobody seems to take responsibility for results, and we have no idea who to blame when things go wrong, or who to appreciate when they benefit us. We do not know where to direct many of the feelings that naturally arise toward those who lead and those who carry out their orders. We do not know how to feel about those who just stand by while unpleasant things happen, and we do not feel good about our own acquiescence. Often what people give to the organization is more kneejerk compliance than heartfelt commitment.

Leaders may claim the same authority they always did when the paradigm that generates belief is impaired, but this claim has a hollow ring, and it leads to frightened acquiescence rather than to committed action. Then it is personal needs and beliefs that produce behavior. It is appetite rather than contribution that moves us, not knowledge of ourselves and the world but opinion defined by our urges.

In this setting the guiding dynamic of the organization is not people working together to preserve and enhance the culture. It is acceptance of what seems inevitable. Crucial concepts such as what is this organization truly here for, what do people need to do in order to thrive, and what are their responsibilities are replaced by such outrageous posturing that people avert their eyes, sleeping through it as much as possible.

Because the legitimate connection between individuals and the group has been damaged, figuring out the big questions falls to the individual and that is an impossible task. People become understandably angry when they are asked to try it. If this system does not engage them or nurture them, at least it seems to provide a buffer between them and uncertainty. They come to accept this situation and to resent any attempt to dislodge them from its protection. The alternative to habit and hiding seems only to be chaos and collapse.

## The Role of Power

Power has to do with getting things done. It is a relationship. More specifically, it is influence. When legitimacy is impaired, it takes more effort for leaders to get other people to do things. During times of transition and the cracking of the old paradigm, "motivation" gets a lot of attention. If you have even glanced in passing at a bookstore window in the past ten years, you know that books about motivation are legion.

Power is one of the basic facts of life; it is ancient and ubiquitous. And it is complex. Its inner force comes in part from habit. When power is strong and clean, people obey out of habit. But not without a healthy component of imagination as well. They feel confident that the influence coming from their leaders is appropriate and they are moved to give of themselves in response. Their genuine thoughts and feelings are contributed to the effort at hand. They can imagine where the impetus for this influence comes from and the benefits if the effort is well executed. Nobody has to tell them to handle the details. Nobody has to tell them to give it all they have got. Nobody has to tell them that if conditions change in mid-operation, they should do what it takes to handle things.

When power is in good shape, it operates like nature herself, in a spontaneous, authentic fashion. The actions that it evokes are part plan and part spontaneity, part rationality and part intuition. But when legitimate power is not robust, imagination is crushed, leaving only habit and expediency to direct us.

To thrive, power must be seen as responsible and appropriate. And during times of change, new understandings are necessary to buttress obedience. Explanations that ring true become important. Setting an appropriate context is essential, and meaningful involvement by those expected to take action must occur.

Does this mean that in order to have legitimate power you must explain where every decision or work order comes from? Or that you must ask everyone who will be affected to vote on it? By no means. Once established, legitimate power runs well on its own as long as honesty and responsibility remain associated with it. When word and deed are closely aligned, power is a relationship that needs no further explanation. It is when power is not legitimate that tedium and resistance enter the equation and then coercion, manipulation, and force are required to produce obedience. Every time.

## The Role of Community

The third misalignment that occurs when the old paradigm is floundering has to do with community. Community is a deep and basic human need. We have a need to know one another, to serve one another, and to be part of something larger than ourselves. Members of a healthy community are awake to their interests and those of the organization. Not ruled by expediency or fear, these people are free to be unique and are able to share moral bonds and limits; they are interested in obedience because it serves them. They are moved by the opportunity to contribute and able to move beyond an obsession with their rights.

But systems in transition where legitimacy is impaired cannot produce this conjunction of qualities. The result is a reduction in the scope of human freedom and responsibility and the dehumanization of leadership. Ideals shrivel; they come down to our own propagation and perpetuation. We look out for number one. In this context employees who are invited to help solve problems as a way of participating in change programs are not going to change anything that matters. And they tend to know it. Unless there is a deep change in the context of the effort, any hope for fruitful participation is false and offers only greater enmeshment in things as they are.

## Waking Up

To break through this configuration the players must move out of isolation and reconnect with the world. The disciplines that encourage personal connection must begin now on a larger scale. Key players can then loosen their ties to dysfunctional relationships and make a connection with the laws of nature and the marketplace where results are determined.

How do you start this? It is clear that nothing changes until it becomes real, and the sort of observation-proof belief that is so entrenched in eras of paradigm shift defies reality, measurement, or trust in our own perceptions. It stops change from being genuinely considered.

Recognition is not an easy step, however. When you think of "getting real," you may think of facing the fact that the results are not there. Sales are down, profit has declined, or the competition is flying on ahead. This, of course, is crucial. But these discoveries by themselves lead to bloodletting, confusion, and a retrenchment into the old beliefs more often than they do to new results.

Don was selling his house, and his real-estate agent was not doing enough. Calls, visits, and even a nasty letter had not done the trick. But he was persistent. He called one day to give Fred an earful, and it was then that the breakthrough happened. His eyes moisten when he recalls it.

Fred answered the phone, and hearing that it was an annoyed Don on the line, said he would have to put him on hold. Laying the phone down, but forgetting to push the hold button, he continued what he had been doing when it rang. What he had been doing was passionately embracing his secretary. It was the work of a minute for them to be lost again in this absorbing activity, and it was not long afterward that the news reached Don's ears. The sound effects were a clear, unambiguous communication and Don lapped it up. He could tell who was with Fred and what each of them was up to. He says they were very expressive. When he had got his fill, but before Fred and his secretary did, Don sprang into action.

"Fred," he yelled through the receiver. "Fred, pick up the phone." And Fred, who had forgotten himself, did so with a start.

"Sorry, Don," he said. "A customer came in and I had to deal with him."

It was here that Don outdid himself. He could have politely ignored what he had heard, but he decided to end the deception and to help Fred see the light and make a choice.

"Let's get real, Fred," said Don. "You weren't talking to a customer. You were making out with your secretary."

Following an embarrassed pause, during which visions of an enraged wife at home danced like malevolent sugarplums in his head, Fred went into action. He became the best real-estate agent Don could have wanted. He took names and dates, he made plans, and he followed through. It was not long before Don's house was sold.

What a great pal Don turned out to be! He helped Fred understand that his hiding was not going to work and that it was time to spring into effective action. And it worked to Don's benefit as well. But do you think that Fred emerged from this a changed man? Did he straighten out his personal entanglements? Did he become an alert and competent real-estate agent? Did he become a true partner, powerful enough to change ineffectiveness and break through resistance? Not for a minute. He became a master at the timely pushing of the hold button.

A shocking revelation is seldom the prod to effective long-term action that it might be, although facing up to the truth is a necessary aspect of regeneration. But we need more than that.

We need to see new possibilities; we need genuine partnership with its meaningful and shared goals. The truth also includes good news: the identification of possibilities, skills, and resources. If we are going to move into action, we need to be engaged in relationships that are safe, honest, and empowering. Regeneration requires a meaningful context that is shared by many people, not frightened isolation.

## Rising Above the Drift

People need to be weaned away from the entanglements of the old system, not assaulted. They will probably have mixed feelings about this activity. Remember that you have been through a similar process in leaving your own internal fortress. You are asking for trouble if you go sailing blindly into the fray, determined to lead the way toward new magnificence and to destroy any behavior you find dysfunctional along the way. Rather, you need to build constructive relationships, focusing on positive, reality-based goals. Dysfunctional activities should not be singled out for special outrage and judgment; they should be given as little attention as possible.

Yet change always stirs up negative feelings that must be worked with. It is wise to encourage people to say what they must about what upsets them. Only after they have unburdened themselves do they have room to listen to a new voice, and to entertain their own interest in taking effective action. Most of us, if permitted to do so, would prefer complaining to making things better. You need to create a process where discussion of ain't it awful is followed by a step-by-step march toward a positive and effective creation of solutions to underlying problems.

A facilitator was working with a sales force that was wildly depressed. Their product had some serious drawbacks. Upper management denied it, but the salespeople were out there with the public on a daily basis and they knew what people were saying. The product was fine. It was not defective or dangerous; it just was not what it could be. It was not, for example, as good as the competition's wares.

These people did not want to hear anyone tell them to get fired up. They were not happy, optimistic, or enthusiastic; they sat with folded arms. So the facilitator began her presentation by speaking to the problem that held them obsessively.

"I just saw a brochure for your product yesterday, and boy was I surprised," she told them. They sat forward in their seats. "Are the pictures accurate? Are those the real colors?" she asked. "Yes," they fairly yelled. "Yes, those are the real goddamned colors." "Even that green?" she asked. "Yes, even that green." Boy did she have their attention. Here at last was someone who knew an ugly color when she saw one. Would she understand how ugly it could be to sell it?

Yes, she could. "That's awful," she shouted. "How do you sell it?" They were thrilled. Someone finally understood. Ten minutes into the seminar and these people were ready to name their children after her.

She told them that they would start the training by working out their relationship to the product. Then she broke them into two groups and had them discuss how bad the product was. No problem there. They entered into this activity heart and soul. Then each group took a turn in front of the room and listed what was wrong with the product. As every detail was spoken, the facilitator instructed the others to yell "That's awful." And yell it they did. They were red faced by the end.

Next the two groups went into session again, and this time their subject was aspects of the product that were acceptable. Not great but all right. As the groups took their turn in front of the room to read off the items on this list, their colleagues were asked to call out "I can sell that." And they did this enthusiastically, too, because it was honest and appropriate. It was their job.

Finally she had the groups reconvene to discuss aspects of the product that were genuinely outstanding and to report them out. When each group read this (much shorter) list, their colleagues were asked to yell "That's great," and this also went well. As long as she understood what they were up against, they could admit that this thing had its good points.

As they prepared to break for lunch, she talked to them about the value of honest acknowledgment followed by decisive action. She suggested that their efforts to get the product improved would stand a better chance of succeeding if they first demonstrated their ability to sell what they had.

They had to show up as the company's partner in order to get the corporate ear.

Was this fair? Not really. But it might be effective, and being indignant had not produced anything. Moreover, she told them, they would discover that if their engagement with this product was honest and committed, that in itself would become a reward. It would lead them to sensible decisions and adaptive behaviors.

Then she gave them the most difficult assignment of the day. During lunch she requested that they have only positive discussions. "Try getting through this meal without complaining—about the food, the service, the product, your boss, and especially about me." They gave it a shot.

They knew what she was up to and it was fine with them. She had demonstrated an understanding for them and their difficulties. She had provided an opportunity for them to vent their feelings and had respected them enough to assume that they wanted to move beyond complaining. The upshot was that by the end of the day she had a group of trusting partners in the sales force, and when upper management heard about the episode, they began discussions with her as well. She became a conduit of information and suggestions between the two. And once they had learned how to talk to one another, they were able to take this dialogue over for themselves. Both sides made some interesting discoveries as a result.

Upper management for the first time was willing to listen to complaints about the product's deficiencies and they made some changes. Then the sales force discovered, to its great surprise, that the change had not made as big a difference as they thought it would. They had gone from trying to sell funny green things they disliked to a skeptical public, to selling funny green things to a new group of people who like that sort of product and appreciated the candid sales approach that the department had developed. The real difference, the salespeople discovered, had come when they began to accept their situation and to take responsibility for it.

The feelings of blame and victimization that dominate working relationships during transitions are addictive. They only come to an end—if they do—when both parties take the cure together. But the cure often starts, as it did with the sales staff, when somebody sees a new possibility and arbitrarily decides to take responsibility for the results, even if they did not create all the conditions that produce them.

To generate new creativity and a greater engagement with work goals, begin with a healthy respect for the feelings of all the people involved. Assume that they must begin to emerge from the effects of an enmeshed relationship before they can shift behavior. You can start this process off quickly and energetically, but you will fail if you naively assume that all you need to do is give people the good news that a new day has arrived.

The real shift will only occur when many people decide to take a look at the relationship between their actions and their results, and the culture of the place begins to reward risk taking, creativity, and responsibility. Then people will participate in the activities that solve problems, and the solutions they discover will align the organization with the emerging environment. This process is an early stage in the development of a new paradigm. The new understandings that begin to emerge at this stage will be created by upstarts, not the keepers of the old flame. These understandings will interest many people. But only when the outlines of this paradigm begin to emerge forcefully will the people in an organization undertake productive activities regularly and on their own.

# 10

## The Nature of Great Organizations

However much we grow or achieve, we are not complete until we are part of a living community. We all need a place in the world where our words and deeds matter. We need to belong to something bigger than we are, a structure that translates us into a larger context, that calls forth aspects of ourselves that have been hidden. We need to participate in the creation of meaningful responses to the events of our times, and to pass value on to those who will follow us. Building an organization where this sense of community flourishes is the end point of all that has gone before in this book.

There are a few obvious prerequisites for such an organization today. We know, for example, that only those organizations that make direct contact with the rapidly shifting facts of life will succeed now, and that they will need to coordinate human relations with a new effectiveness in order to achieve their ends. We also know that this amounts to a transformation in the way organizations do their work and that trying to achieve this through a change program or two is senseless.

We know, in addition, that unless the social order makes a similar shift, the organizations that manage this transformation will waste a lot of effort fighting inertia and opposition. They will not get the resources they need, the employees they deserve, or the markets they seek. The new paradigm discovered by these organizations must become the new paradigm shared by everyone.

The workplace will be a primary site for this personal and public transformation. Business organizations hold most of the wealth and influence in the modern world; they are pervasive at a time when other institutions have withered. Society and individuals cannot make the shifts they need to in defiance of these dominating organizations. If they encourage sleep, deception, and lassitude, those qualities will pervade our lives.

Nor do we need to discover different paradigms for personal, business, and social life. All organizations are a force of nature; they are created by its laws. Business organizations are not immune to these laws; nor are the people working in them different from their neighbors. The laws that make a business function well are the same laws that foster individual and social growth. The paradigm that contains one set of laws will contain all of them. This has always been true, and when it seems otherwise, when the good of the individual and the social order are at odds, the paradigm has fallen out of alignment and is in decline.

These great organizations will teach us how to live. They will organize our efforts to deploy resources creatively and effectively in a world that appears to be indifferent to our needs and is moving at breakneck speed. They will help us accommodate rapid change and diversity. They will be the vehicles of personal and social transformation.

Is this an untenable hope? Is it naive? It may be. But it is a compelling goal, one that is big enough to fire the engines of transition and powerful enough to move us out of isolation, to get us playing hard and honestly. It can move us to discover what is truly possible, so that we bring into being ways of living and working that presently seem unimaginable.

## The Power of Imagination

The transforming device called forth by great organizations comes down to imagination. Nearly five hundred years ago Copernicus changed the prevailing paradigm about the relationship of the Earth to the universe. The most basic understandings of life were transformed because we became convinced that the Earth was not the center of the universe, but a planet orbiting a middle-sized star. In locating new and more accurate laws of the universe, laws that were discovered through imagination, Copernicus set the stage for a chain of discoveries about the laws of the world and humankind.

What Copernicus described was a universe that could be imagined but not directly seen. His work reminds us that there are no laws out there that are not in us. The relationships between energy and matter that determine the laws of the stars are those that generate and sustain human life. The laws we discover through space exploration, or through medical research, are located through our imaginations. That is how medicine works. That is why polling predicts elections. That is why space flight and landing on the moon are possible. We carry the laws of the universe within ourselves. We sense them because their truths reside in us.

A sense of fascination and adventure is essential to the continuation of human life. So, too, is a willingness to extend ourselves and to make contact. These are all aspects of imagination. They put us in touch with ideas that are as true and powerful as the abstractions of natural science are. They make relationships work and great organizations function. Without them we do not adjust and advance. We must learn again to value the abstractions that have transformed institutions in great cultures of the past.

## The Culture

The personal awareness developed through the practices that lead to self-knowledge opens up wonderful internal resources. It is the foundation for the knowledge-based relationships that move people into the realm of action, past the dissatisfaction and self-doubt that impede movement, beyond the search for who they are and into a territory where they challenge the inertia in life. Here they take the initiative to create, extend, repair, and experience what life has in store for them.

Those who do this are acting publicly. Without necessarily intending it, they create a public space in which their spontaneous responses to life's challenges may be understood by others. What they are moved to do in this arena will strike a chord of recognition in many people. When they act according to their deepest stirrings in this public space, the results are gratifying.

Meeting the challenges of the times means acknowledging that it is our turn to take this initiative, to make the contribution that is in us, and to make it in a way that directly engages the crucial problems we face. But this work cannot be done alone or even in small groups. It requires wise and coherent organizations that assist us to move into effective action.

Certain difficult-to-define factors determine which organizations do this well and which do not. Great organizations tend to have ample resources and considerable wealth, but it is the intangible characteristics that make effective action possible. Imagination is one of them. Belief is another. These characteristics produce a healthy culture that effectively aligns an organization and its members with its environment.

Every great organization has a culture that generates involvement and action. It contains the seeds of trust, unity, and confidence. It teaches traditions, techniques, and ways of being that people could not learn in any other manner. It tells us about the work and sacrifice that it took to get us where we are, speaks of the loves and enjoyment that were generated. It produces practical responses to the world that protect, support, and enliven people. We learn things in this context that we cannot learn anyplace else, and we perform acts here that we cannot perform on our own. It is the foundation for our best contribution. A great organization is much more than the sum of its parts.

## The Foundation

If culture is at the heart of great organizations, at the core of culture lies an agreement. In order for the culture to survive the challenges it will face, the agreement needs to be a genuine expression of the sentiments of the members, grounded in truths that everyone acknowledges. This agreement must be concrete and measurable and strong enough to move people into action that is in honest alignment with its standards. And if some people are excluded from this agreement, there will be instability and incompleteness in the adjustment mechanisms of the organization. There will be internal territories that remain unexplored and mysterious, territories that will not yield their treasures and from which confusion and surprise will emanate.

This agreement requires that we acknowledge being more than an aggregate of people who happen to live in proximity to one another. It stipulates the rights and duties of membership, the relationship between leaders and members and the nature of authority. It is a public declaration that spells out what the organization stands for, its mission and goals, as well as its rules and standards and the actions it will promote. The work of exploring, clarifying, and coalescing support for these agreements must take place or the system will be hollow and unproductive. No plan or strategy, no infusion of talent or capital will make a significant difference until this is well under way.

The process of establishing a foundation starts with looking for the agreement that lives in the organization as it stands now. We must be willing to know what is there and what is missing. We must overcome the fear that we will not like what we discover. A true agreement can always be located; producing canned, inauthentic agreements is foolish.

## The Rituals

Because intangible factors such as belief and imagination determine the nature and success of an organization, activities that engage the spirit, emotions, and thoughts of people will be essential to a new culture. A central component of any successful culture is the rituals that relate individuals to the world in a productive way. These rituals make the accumulated wisdom of the group available to its members. They touch peoples' intellects and spirits, moving them more deeply than rules, fears, or proddings do, more profoundly than the surface concerns and conflicts that grip and paralyze them. Rituals align people with their honest feelings, with others in the group, and with the needs of the organization. They are powerful tools that build strength and continuity, immense resources that are seldom tapped.

An effective culture engages its members so deeply that they spontaneously take responsibility for its effectiveness and survival. They trust it to guide their daily activities. Its rituals do much to create this situation. They prepare people for the harmonious assumption of increasing responsibility through an educating process that teaches them, and the system itself, to be honest, to take action, and to adjust constantly. They create an ethic and a problem-solving mechanism that works. Societies depend on this process for their survival. So do work organizations.

Effective modern organizations ask their members to do more than obey rules, however. They need people with a faculty for independent observation and free thinking, an ability to assess the possibilities of the environment and of themselves in it. Evaluating, creating, and adjusting are crucial characteristics of productive employees today. The culture and rituals of a wise organization promise a personal fulfillment that is greater than self-absorption. A change agent who wants to move an organization from dependency toward a regeneration will look for rituals that symbolize both personal and organizational transition, that relate the real needs of the organization to the real lives of its members.

> The management team of a mid-sized department store was charged with the task of creating a turnaround. Profits had been declining for several years, morale was low, and corporate office was breathing down their necks. They felt there was nothing they could do to make the place more profitable and they were running scared.
>
> As a consequence they did what most people in situations such as this do: they fought with one another. They played tricks, they hid resources, and they found someone to blame for everything that went wrong. They snapped at employees and treated them like children, and although they worked very hard, the slide got worse.
>
> At length they began to face the fact that they had hit bottom and nobody was going to help. So they began to search for something they could do that would make a difference. They asked themselves where they could improve performance even if corporate did not support them and

they came up with the idea of quality. They could provide outstanding service to customers. They could train their staffs to care and to perform. This would help business and it would not require much help from the top. It was an exciting idea.

But when they took a good look around, they sank back in despair. Their employees were not the most carefully chosen, highly paid, and trained people in the business. They were overwhelmed by their workloads, often at each other's throats, and not happy to be where they were. They complained about work schedules, about inadequate equipment, about the way the place looked, and, for the most part, they did not like their bosses. Turning this around would be no easy task. But they had nothing to lose, so they decided to go for it.

They began by going off on a three-day retreat. In this quiet setting, away from phones and all the conflicting demands, far from the noise and familiar surroundings, they could calm down, take a breath, and get clear. They held frank discussions about what was not working. They looked one another in the eyes and told the truth as they saw it.

They also became clear on what worked, and they told each other what they wanted to achieve. They discovered that they shared many values, many hopes and fears and dreams. They saw how much they had been hurting others and uncovered an ability to care that had been just below the surface through all the warfare. They were impressed and they were moved.

As they discovered this affection, they began looking for words to describe the vision they shared. Finding those words was not difficult, and it was enlivening. They created a compelling mission statement that delighted them, and they came up with a set of work goals that would make this mission live. They decided to take their unified vision back to the office and share it with everyone. They would use it to lead the charge toward a new quality of service.

But sitting in this pleasant place, telling the truth as if it were about to become extinct, they quickly spotted the problem. A plan of this sort would mean drastically changing the culture of the company. This was not a simple program; it was the dawning of a new age and nobody was likely to follow their lead. If they went back and told everyone how much they had come to respect one another, employees would laugh to themselves. They had seen the infighting and the blaming, and they were unlikely to trust their leaders to act differently just because of a retreat. And when it came to being inspired by these leaders to think and work in a new way? Not a chance.

How could they carry this new discovery back to work with them? How could they build the urge to follow that came to leaders who held a share of mind with their employees? There was only one way: Become outrageous.

So they planned a show. They would present their vision, their new goals and work standards to the department heads at a meeting where they would demonstrate, not talk about, their new way of working. It would be such a surprise, that at the very least, people would have to wonder if a new day were not in fact genuinely dawning. It would be a ritual and also the best business meeting they could produce.

The meeting would begin much like any other. They would sit in front of the assembled employees at a long table. Flip charts would proclaim their vision and goals and they would take turns discussing what it all meant. But then they would do something amazing. Without announcing it, they would slip into a secretly rehearsed skit. Appearing to continue the discussion, they would make snide remarks to one another, quibbling and goading. They would do what they often did in less-public settings. Each of them would depict themselves at their worst.

Fresh out of their retreat and all its honest talk, they were quite clear about how they acted when they wanted to be obnoxious. This was easy to portray, and the more they rehearsed, the more they came to enjoy consciously exposing these personal characteristics. One manager was imperious and snide, another was defensive and blustery; one was a stickler for absurd detail, another accused the others of not living up to agreements. All of them were self-righteous and rigid. They would demonstrate how it had been, how they had been. This would not be another meeting where the top guys preached to the troops about change but left themselves out of it. It would be a living demonstration of their own transformation.

It worked like a charm. On the day of the meeting the department heads fell for everything. They were impressed by the meeting, they liked the vision, and they believed that the argument was for real. Only when the executive brawl got out of hand and their leaders left the room angrily one by one did it begin to dawn on the staff that it was a sting. They loved it. They whooped, they clapped, and they laughed. They had never seen anything like it in their lives. They were enjoying themselves immensely.

While the leaders were out of the room, a meeting facilitator engaged them in discussion. What had they seen? Was it anything they had seen before?

Seen it? They had felt it, many times right in the teeth.

Why were the leaders doing this?

To show us what we do.

No. To show you what they do. To let you know that they are wise to their own patterns, and that they know how difficult it will be to change.

But they have been learning something else, continued the facilitator. They have been learning how to clear up breakdowns. They have been practicing the art of speaking honestly to one another about what is not working, getting back in touch with the vision that unites them, and moving back on track. "In fact," said the facilitator, "they could be out in the hall right now doing that. For all we know they could be about to come back in here completely transformed, ready to change a bunch of words into action."

And with that the management team burst into the room. Transformed.

In a nearby lounge they had been frantically putting on tights and jumping into large duck costumes. These costumes, with their great fuzzy yellow bodies, huge bow ties, and massive plastic feet, had no special significance beyond the fact that they were the most amusing ones available at the costume shop. All week long secret rehearsals had produced rounds of laughter as duck ran into duck; at homes dogs had learned to run for cover when duck feet were brought out for extra practice.

But now, masters of their disguises, they were the essential artful ducks as they danced into the room to the music of Patti LaBelle singing "New Attitude." To gleeful cheers from the staff, they danced up the aisles and across the front. They danced with one another and they danced with employees. And as the music ended, they danced out of the room holding up placards that read It's Time for a Change. It was some time before the staff stopped whooping.

When the leaders returned a few minutes later in civilian clothes, they were greeted by a standing ovation. Each of them spoke now, out of costume and from the heart. I did this, they all said in one way or another, because I care very much about the success of this program. I know what it will take to make a change of this magnitude. I know the change must begin with me.

This unusual experience, which engaged everyone in activities that called to all their senses, had created a possibility. A new public space had begun to appear where words and deeds might begin to have more integrity. If the management team followed through on its promise to lead according to its vision, the foundation for a new relationship between them and the staff was possible. It would require great discipline and much hard work. Departments would have to look honestly at themselves and determine their vision, goals, and standards. New agreements would need to be forged and new habits developed. But it was a good start. They had made a commitment to begin a transition, and to begin with themselves. They had taken a public stand in a way that could be measured and evaluated. They were very happy.

## Building New Authority

If such a new beginning is to succeed, it must be followed by the best that people can give. It will work only if those engaged in it are moving actively along their own individual road of self-knowledge—their philosopher's road map. Every possible temptation to lose focus will present itself, every form of breakdown will occur. People will grow tired and upset, confused and suspicious. But even a partial success is rewarding because it gives birth to a new system of authority.

If imagination transforms organizations, encouraging movement, alertness, adaptive goals, and strategies, belief is also vital. It fosters obedience, confidence, coordination, and perseverance. Healthy belief is a form of authority that tells people how to perceive life, how to perform tasks and solve problems. The qualities of authority include assurance, guidance, discipline, and good judgment. Properly constructed authority is a form of internalized belief that leads to order, creativity, and freedom, and it teaches people how to care for one another.

Because it always involves obedience, it is commonly mistaken for coercion, but genuine authority is not coercive. Where force is used, authority has failed and relationships will be unstable. The obedience implied in authority is voluntary obedience. It is the conscious response of someone who is acting in his or her best interest, who is moved by the authority, feels larger because of it, is able to act with authenticity and spontaneity within its bounds.

Authority takes some time to develop because it grows out of common experiences. It is an interpretive process requiring subtlety, acceptance of ambiguity, and an awareness of interdependence. People who share in such a system are likely to be alert and awake. They see problems emerging and cheerfully set about to solve them. They see opportunities where others see only routine or barriers. They anticipate one another and move harmoniously together.

There are many ways to move toward the creation of new authority in an organization. It is not necessary to slip into costumes the way the management team did. The rituals that herald its arrival can be new and inventive, or they can be based on quarterly reports, departmental meetings, or other common events. They should take a form that is natural to the people engaged in it. Whatever form they take, however, they always need to involve human-centered activities that are vision-focused and public, activities where everyone takes appropriate responsibility for sensible results and where words can be measured against deeds.

For a month following the management team's duck dance, the whole organization was engaged in a fever of activity.

Department heads, following the instructions they had been given at the meeting, set up a program of their own. Its purpose was to get into every corner of the organization, to learn what strength employees had, to learn how they solved the practical problems of their workday, how they were able to do without enough resources, how they handled uncertainty and technical problems, and how they overcame cultural conflict. It would locate the agreement that already existed and identify its strengths.

Like the seers and artists who rejuvenate transitional cultures, these people would find the voice of the new organization. It would be a realistic voice that grew out of their knowledge of the daily problems that must be overcome if truly new results were going to emerge. It would eventually join with the voice of the people who made the strategic decisions, generating a new vision and discipline that systematically called to the best in everyone.

Each department was given written material to use in creating a unified context for this search. The charge was to come back with a vision, goals, standards, requests, and promises, all attached to deadlines. It was a lot of work and it required a level of involvement and responsibility that was new to them. Some joined in enthusiastically, others were slow to do so, and some resisted mightily. But the momentum grew and by month's end, the results were remarkable.

A presentation of each department's work would be made at a ceremony attended by the whole staff. They were asked to create a three-minute video that delineated their vision and goals in their own way, projecting their departmental culture in the process. Going public, taking a stand, and asking to be measured according to their own standards fascinated most of them, especially in the light of the stories about the duck dance. Their video was an opportunity to participate in a similar event themselves.

With help from a facilitator, department heads worked their departments, discussing the nature of the assignment, identifying strengths and weaknesses, creating visions that were task specific, preparing goals and standards. They said to one another, if we are going to succeed, this is how we must work together and here is how we will measure our results. They grew anxious to put it on the screen, show themselves at work, to express themselves.

When the day of the event arrived, the excitement was palpable as employees filed into the ballroom and the lights dimmed. Every department's video was different. One, known as the least customer oriented, did a skit that depicted them being rude to customers, and they presented their vision, goals, and standards as a pledge to turn this around. The audience loved it; it created a sensation and set an example. People who had been looked down on were now looked to with interest, and they would be watched for results. Their colleagues would enforce these standards because this department's annoyed customers created problems for everybody. These expectations would not come from bosses alone, but from peers and from their own awakened sense of possibility.

Members of a department that was predominantly Spanish speaking felt it was imperative that their statement indicate this. Their vision was presented by the popular assistant department head who spoke with diffidence, charm, and pride. In the video her colleagues stood behind her, cheering her assertion of identity, her challenge, and request for belonging.

Another department was in great disarray and unable to come up with a compelling statement. Their video became a marker of where they were and how far they had to go. People in this department could measure for themselves where they stood in relation to other departments. This realization had an impact on them. It was the starting point for the creation of a new work culture.

Yet another department was known as the best in the organization, and they were proud of it. Their statement was simple and confident and their video depicted them at work, enjoying themselves.

Each video was made in the work setting, demonstrating to others in the organization what they did, who the people in the department were, and the personality of the group. Other employees could see people and functions they had not known about and develop a new understanding of the breadth of the organization to which they belonged. When it was over, the lights came on to a tumultuous reception. The whole staff was elated. They had shown themselves off, seen their colleagues clearly, and they all had taken a public stand.

Then the members of the management team handed out framed copies of each department's vision statement to be put on a wall, and they noted when they would reconvene. They made it clear that they would measure results, celebrate victories, and make adjustments. And before disbanding they reminded the employees that as they went back to their workstations, alive with possibilities, committed as never before, they could expect breakdowns and confusion. This, they noted, should not be worrisome. The vision on the wall would guide them, and so would their goals and work standards, along with the new pride and problem-solving techniques they had learned in the process of creating their statements.

When it gets difficult, they told the employees, we have a request. It is embodied in a song, and over the loudspeaker system came the strains of Ben E. King singing "Stand by Me." As the music played, members of the management team moved forward, took the hands of the employees, and danced in a circle around the room. It would be up to everyone to hold to the standards and to create adjustments. It would be up to the leaders to make it clear through their example that this would mean hard work and discipline. It was not a pep rally, or a game designed by the people at the top to force those below them to do more. It was a pledge of community, authority, and the generation of new value. It was a step toward a new level of alertness, a new spirit of coordination, and a new relationship to results.

Activities such as this also become an exercise in meaning what you say. If you do not mean it, do not try it. If you do it in order to manipulate people into complying with you, it will blow up in your face. Once you have stood up in a public arena whose territory you have helped define and told people what you value, and what you may be counted on to contribute, nothing is ever the same again. You may not succeed, but you cannot go back to the old ways either. People will not let you.

The duck dance and vision videos are a process where rituals are found that tie people to belief and imagination, the intangibles that create great organizations. They evoke the emotional support that connects leaders to groups, and individuals to the practical realities of the organization and the marketplace. In doing this they deal in spirit as well as in specifics: how you do your job, work out conflicts, coordinate with other departments, handle cultural diversity. The employees are the shock troops who have gathered the data. Change agents have only to organize this information, create a place for it, and nurture it. They legitimize these work processes and make them a part of the new belief system.

In this community people may at last reveal who they are by responding with their best efforts to life's challenges. What they do and say matters here. It is a theater where actions are matched with deeds for everyone to see, a place where shared goals are discovered and from which action may spring.

Such an organization will naturally take its place in the larger community because it can respond competently to the great questions of the times. Its energized, alert members will understand their greater social responsibilities; they will recognize an interdependence that extends beyond the organization. As they undertake this new work, they are magnified through participation in the life and destiny of the larger social order. They make a contribution, solve real problems, and invent new ways of living productively. They touch a broader tradition, one of human bravery, action, and beauty. They touch the truths of cultures past and the possibilities of those to come.

## Creating Enduring Value

Once this great organization is built, we have reached the safe shore where wisdom, creativity, and excellence reign and then we can rest, correct? Wouldn't *that* be nice. But human life is not like that. In the first place, we never achieve it all. Even Plato, who has been abused for several thousand years as a wild-eyed idealist, said that this state of affairs would never come to be and that this fact does not matter. It does not matter because getting there, going at it full tilt, is the glory of human life.

We cannot achieve permanent excellence. We cannot alter the cycles that define human life. Greatness achieved eventually moves into decline. Sit with Socrates in the morning, and you are foolish again by the afternoon; create a magnificent organization, and it hits the skids by the time the books praising it are arranged in the store windows. The goal of a great culture and a great organization is to thrive on this knowledge and to align with these cycles. Great organizations do not fix on one way of being or doing things. They see the possibilities that live at the moment and they create the best possible experiences, goods, and services. They produce the value that is appropriate to the season and then they move to the next one.

When we understand the natural movement of the cycles in the organization and in the marketplace, we are able to devise products and services that are appropriate and useful. We gather the resources that are necessary for the creation and delivery of these goods. We are at peace with ourselves and with those with whom we work. And when we recall that the creation that seeks to stay where it was born, or even to remain at its height, never makes its full contribution, we are able to turn our attention to what comes next and not to fight the moving cycles. When we live and work this way, life does not seem malevolent.

The challenge and the possibility of the times are great. But we do not face this condition unarmed. Our ancestors confronted similar challenges with courage and liveliness, and they solved many of their problems in a way that has value for us. Once we have joined the ancient dialogue, accepting the gift of our inheritance from it, it becomes clear that we are neither in over our heads nor alone. Waking up and looking around we will discover that complex and powerful currents move inside us. We will see that this is true of others as well, and that great deeds are being done. We will recognize heroes in our midst.

I have introduced you to some of my heroes in this book. The Ice Queen made courageous discoveries and responded heroically to them; so did Betty and Karl, Fairway Fred and Pat, and so did the woman who was called The Bitch. Those who looked at the truth, who dared greatly, and achieved all that was available to achieve are heroes.

A hero goes on a great journey, overcomes difficult obstacles, answers unfair riddles, and is not turned back by fear and misunderstanding. Heroes seldom achieve the goal they start out seeking, but they come back transformed and bring the community a great gift. The hero's gift, whatever it is, always transforms the community in turn, and when we encounter them, we must accept their gifts. As we do this our spirit rises up to meet them, we participate in a transformation, we live our lives more fully, and we enjoy ourselves. Then we may build on the gift, joining with others to create enduring value.

Alexis de Tocqueville observed more than 150 years ago that "the past has ceased to throw its light upon the future and the mind of man wanders in obscurity." He was right. But that light has not gone out. It lives in the torch handed to us by the heroes we come to know. By accepting the torch we may discover the will to proceed and the knowledge of how to do it. Through it we uncover remembrance, love, contribution, and strength. We remember what we know and have always known, and the knowledge we uncover this way gives us permission to seek meaning and to take action.

Throughout history, time and again, people have risen up unexpectedly from crisis and confusion to create magnificent life forms. When they did this great cities flourished, the arts and medicine were transformed, science and commerce made unlooked-for advances. During these times, wise and complex institutions emerged that guided people through the vicissitudes of life. And in the face of fear and denial, people remembered to value themselves and to care for one another. This is a great human tradition. It is our inheritance. And now it is our work.

# Index